SALES SURVIVAL

MORE FROM GORDON O'NEILL

For more information, services, products, and blog, please visit:

www.sales-survival.com

Download the *Sales Survival* app for your smartphone today at:

Apple App Store & Google Android Market

Contact Gordon O'Neill and the *Sales Survival* team:

gordon@sales-survival.com

SALES SURVIVAL

Your complete guide to a career in sales, including effective communication, sales techniques, customer retention, marketing strategies, and becoming *the professional salesperson.*

GORDON P. O'NEILL

Bootstrap
Books
Publishing

ISBN: ISBN-13 978-0-986-9583-0-4

Gordon O'Neill
Visit my website at www.Sales-Survival.com or contact me: gordon@sales-survival.com

Printed in the United States of America
First Printing: August 2011
For information about this title, contact the publisher:

Bootstrap Books Publishing
RR #1
41 Beamish Rd.
Hastings, Ontario
K0L 1Y0

publisher@bootstrapbookspublishing.com

O'Neill, Gordon

    Sales Survival: Your complete guide to a career in sales including effective communication, sales techniques, customer retention, marketing strategies, and becoming the professional salesperson./Gordon O'Neill – 1st ed.

    Includes index

        1.   Sales Training. 2. Effective Sales Communication. 3. Effective Selling.
        4. Self-Help/Business

Printed in the United States of America

10 9 8 7 6 5 4 3 2 1   11 12 13

To everyone who has been told "it is impossible" or "it can't be done". Dare to be different, and prove them wrong.

ACKNOWLEDGEMENTS

What a journey. We're finally here. Writing this book has really given me a new perspective on life and a true appreciation for the people in it.

I would like to start by thanking my wife, Shannon. Through thick and thin, she has always believed in me and been right beside me every step of the way. When I have hit a wall of self doubt, Shannon has been the one who has lifted my spirits and given me the true passion to succeed. Without her, this book would never have reached the store shelves. Shannon is my best friend, my lover, and my everything. Thank you, Sunshine—I love you with all of my heart.

I thank my father, Patrick, who has always supported me; through my childhood, he was my hero and my rock. As the "ultimate salesman," he taught me that when it comes to selling, you are only a clown in a three-ring circus. "If they like the act, they will buy the show". Thanks for everything, Dad.

I thank Trevor Stevens, who helped me put my thoughts to paper. Stay focused on what you believe in, and chase your dreams. Thank you for all your help.

I thank Paul Stevens, for being a sounding board to bounce my ideas off while providing solid industry publishing knowledge and support.

I thank Nellie Smith for her editorial expertise.

I would also like to thank all of my previous managers and bosses. Through good and bad leadership, you all helped shape my career path and mould me into the sales expert that I have become. Thank you, everyone, for your encouragement, support, and even the discipline.

I would like to recognize one of my previous managers in particular—Jim Ellis. Thank you, Jim, for finding a diamond in a cow field, cleaning off all the bullshit, and helping me to shine. I thank you for all of the life lessons that you taught me and the continual "career profiling" that you did for me when I worked within your organization.

I have been truly blessed to have a great support group, and I thank everyone who has been a part of this journey.

I hope you all enjoy reading this book as much as I enjoyed writing it.

SOLD

You Just Bought My Book!

You just became my newest customer.

I just want to take a moment to thank you for your business. I appreciate the fact that you spent your hard-earned cash to purchase this book. You also just made an investment in your sales career and your future, and I would like to congratulate you on your wise selection.

For all the customers I serve through my coaching practice, speaking events, volunteer activities, and through writing *Sales Survival*, I have three simple goals:

1. To help people be successful
2. To establish long-term, value-added relationships
3. To enjoy life

My goal in writing this book was to make it so useful that you would want to refer 10 of your friends to buy my book. Please let me know if I reached my goal with you.

Because of YOU, and each of my valued customers, I have the opportunity to do what I love—sell, write, speak, coach, and teach.

THANK YOU!

Please feel free to comment at: **feedback@sales-survival.com**

SALES SURVIVAL CHALLENGE

Pledge to take this challenge and see the results!

❑ I, _____, commit to reading this book from cover to cover.

❑ I will implement the proven teachings and methods in this book in order to be more effective in my sales career and life.

❑ I commit to continually working on my strengths and identifying my weaknesses.

❑ I will always sell in an ethical manor and will put MY customer's needs first.

❑ I will become a *professional salesperson.*

❑ I will be SUCCESSFUL.

❑ I will listen to my customers and build long-term, value-added relationships.

❑ I will support my colleagues and help them develop their careers.

❑ I will be passionate about my career.

❑ I will be the top salesperson in my company.

❑ I will follow my dreams and live my best life.

Cut this challenge out, and keep it with you wherever you sell. Use this challenge as a commitment to live by, a professional oath of sorts, a starting point for the foundation of your success. Use each chapter of this book as a list of techniques to master. With this winning combination, you *will* succeed.

INTRODUCTION

Hello, and welcome to the best investment you'll ever make as an effective salesperson. You may have the nice suit, the shiny shoes, the expensive-looking watch, and the pretty gold name tag. You may have experience and charm and a nice, big, bright smile.

But unless you've got a full stock of openers, closers, enforcers, and other weapons of influence, you will never fully thrive in your job or business. Charm is charm, and a gimmick is a gimmick, but these only get your foot in the door (I'm sorry to say). Unless you've got product and social/situational awareness to accompany it, you're just another smiling face—as opposed to a reliable asset to your customer's consuming needs.

In this book, you will learn how to be just that: a valuable aid in your customer's decision-making process. You will not be just another suit. You will learn how to influence and direct your clientele in the direction of what you want to sell, as opposed to what they came to buy. I'm not just talking about helping people make the purchase.

I'm talking about selling.

Most consumers see you as help—a means through which to buy. You are the checkout person at the front of the store, or even the catalogue they receive in the mail. You are a tool at their disposal, good for following directions and answering calls. Sad to say, most salespeople feel this way about themselves, as well. Anybody can help the customer find what they came to buy; you just have to know where things are.

It takes a professional to surpass those original expectations and direct attention to something more specific, to something better—to a superior, perhaps more costly, item that they either weren't aware of previously or hadn't considered appropriately before your attention.

Every salesperson talks. Few salespeople make their buyers listen.

From filling quotas to customer fulfilment, maximizing profits to minimizing error margins, this book will round off your edges as an agent of your company (and maybe even sharpen a few). It will build your confidence in the field and make you more aware of what is happening during the different stages of a sale. You will better understand the mechanics of the interactions you likely already have on a consistent basis, and very quickly, you will see the bumps in your everyday interactions even out.

If you have bought this book already, congratulations! You just did yourself a big favour.

If you are in a bookstore considering it, I'd suggest you check your wallet. Don't worry if you don't have cash—they probably take credit where you are.

CONTENTS

CHAPTER ONE

KEY SELLING STRATEGIES

A human being should be able to change a diaper, plan an invasion, butcher a hog, conn a ship, design a building, write a sonnet, balance accounts, build a wall, set a bone, comfort the dying, take orders, give orders, cooperate, act alone, solve equations, analyze a new problem, pitch manure, program a computer, cook a tasty meal, fight efficiently, die gallantly. Specialization is for insects.
—*Robert A. Heinlein*

The showroom can be a strange and terrible place for any inexperienced sales representative, as can any equivalent in any selling environment. Your bullpen, your office, your telecommunications centre—they are all signs that you've made it. You have the job—the people above have trusted you enough to be their smiling face and firm handshake. Now you've got to come through with the goods. Not only the entire range of your income, but your very job depends on the performance you put forward. Do you have the guts? You likely do, because you're already

Do you have the methodology to succeed?

wearing that expensive suit we talked about earlier. But do you have the methodology to succeed?

PRODUCT KNOWLEDGE

It is vital that you know your product. There is nothing less impressive than a man or woman talking endlessly about something they know nothing about whatsoever. They flail about and grasp at straws, taking long pauses to conjure garbage they don't mean, for people they don't actually like. This is transparent, and they can fully expect to be identified and persecuted through the paralyzing means of interrogation by the customer and eventual loss of the sale. Any person facing an insistent customer demanding answers they don't have and presenting issues beyond their depth will become flustered and aggravated (with) themselves. There is absolutely no way to sell something in this day and age unless you understand the particulars of it—at least not safely.

> There is nothing less impressive than a man or woman talking endlessly about something they know nothing about whatsoever.

Let me tell you why that is: the customer is smart. He has access to the Internet, books, and product brochures. Not only that, but your employers spend millions of dollars yearly putting out excellent advertising to keep the customer informed. Nine times out of ten, the customer is more informed than the salesperson. The age of slick smiles and greasy hair are long over, friend, and all that's left now are hard facts and firm knowledge—the grand majority of which have come right from the source.

Most conventional sales tactics were formed in the earlier decades of this century, and the fact that they've endured this long proves their validity. They've grown and been polished and augmented, but generally speaking they've remained the same. And while our fathers (or sometimes more accurately, ancestors) have been sharpening their techniques down to razor-sharp points through the years, the world around us has changed radically in a very short period of time—and those very techniques I'm referring to have been adamantly insistent on not following suit. This is unfortunate, but try to keep a level head, for we are not doomed. You will find through further reading that these new and unprecedented generations have been busy at work cultivating our own strain of more developed approaches. We now count on our customers being fluent in our language, our "doublespeak" (term is from George Orwell's *1984*), and the ready-and-waiting customer (in his most extreme form) is something that is becoming more real by the day. Your customer will understand the products. He has done some

> Your customer will understand the products. He has done some basic reading and is coming to you for the real numbers, the specifics.

basic reading and is coming to you for the real numbers, the specifics. If you don't have them, well, he will tend to just roll off and go someplace else to find somebody who does.

Start with the brochures. Get basic ideas about the products. Talk to other salespeople, more experienced veterans who've been there for a while. The wonderful thing about people who are good at what they do is that they like to talk about their success. They will share their knowledge and regale you with stories of times when they did everything right (sometimes to no end), because most of them are fairly full of themselves and enjoy being looked up to. If you need any proof, take a look at what I'm doing *right now!*

> I am recommending that you leave the majority of your social life for after work.

The point is: if you want to know, the sources are out there. You just need to take the time to tap into them. I would recommend spending fifteen minutes a day reading over the available materials for whatever it is you're selling. You probably spend more time than that *socializing* around your office. I loved all the people at my first dealership—they made me want to go to work in the morning. But as I started to mature as a salesperson, I came to realize that, while they were pleasant human beings, those people weren't paying my bills. I'm definitely not recommending you snub your co-workers, but I am recommending that you leave the majority of your social life for after work. For that matter, invite the people you like at work over for dinner, or go out for coffee. Strengthen those bonds, and become more than just an acquaintance. You never know when those bonds might help you—at work or on any level.

It is your job to know a bit about everything—you are not a specialist (see above quote for inspiration and vindication), and as a jack of all trades, it will be your responsibility to get it right, whatever that means. If you want to stay afloat, you have to have a wide range of information about all the products you hope to sell. The only real option aside from that is to pass the customer off to somebody who does know—and that's money out of your pocket.

But it's also a selling strategy.

HONESTY

Honesty is key. I absolutely cannot stress this point enough! If you're caught in a lie, if a potential customer even *smells* a lie, you will lose credibility instantly, and credibility is our universal currency. It is impossible to make a sale if your customer doesn't feel he can believe what you say. As a professional salesperson, it is your job, above all, to make that customer understand that you are a credible and reliable salesperson. If you lie, cheat,

> Credibility is our universal currency.

and steal your way through your first couple of months, you might cram in those extra sales and make a bit of a name for yourself (assuming you're an excellent liar and luck is perpetually on your side). But if sales is a career for you, you need a solid track record and substratum of good tips and recommendations that truly work to your benefit. You're building your career from the ground up, and a strong foundation of honesty is absolutely *fundamental*. If you can't make a sale today, you might make one a year from now, just because that person remembered you were straight with him. You will not remember every single person that comes across your desk—but if you display honesty, patience, and hard work, they will absolutely remember *you*.

As a new seller starting off, you'll need to get to know your new environment. You will need time to get a grasp on your new surroundings, and understand exactly what your job is—period. Anyone who imagines you are a whiz right off the bat is assuming too much. So, as a new, inexperienced salesperson, what do you do with that customer who wants accurate, concise, and specific help—and wants it *now?* There will always be people who are not satisfied with anything short of perfection, and they see any hesitation as incompetence and uselessness. Customers demand honesty and worldliness, and they fully expect you to lie. They are on full alert, at all times, waiting for you to slip up or give them information they know is false. So what do you do?

> If you can't make a sale today, you might make one a year from now, just because that person remembered you were straight with him.

When I was new to the game, and somebody wanted answers I didn't have, I would tell them, flat out: "Mr. and Mrs. Customer, I don't know. But I'll find out for you." It was a lesson I learned the hard way. I've had times when I was midway through the month and I hadn't put out any cars. It was because I was pushing, and clients would pick up on my anxious mood through my frantic probing. More than that, it was because I was lying and making things up, and the customer could tell I was being evasive and untruthful. People are wary creatures. I was doing everything I could to make a name for myself, and I'd wind up back at my desk over lunch, just sitting there, thinking to myself, "I just lied to those people."

It wasn't a good feeling then, and it's not pleasant to remember it now. What it came down to, in the end, was whether or not I really wanted that to be my job.

> Selling is about knowing what the customers want and what you have to give them.

Do you want to spend the rest of your life lying to people?

The answer for me, of course, was no. Do I want to lie to people? Do I want to feel on the spot, all the time? Or do I want to focus on developing my skills and learning how to do my job right? Selling isn't just about gut instinct and verbal reflex, although those are often your right and left hands. It's about knowing what the customers want and what you have to give them.

BE COMPETITIVE (GO WHERE THE MONEY IS)

At an early stage in my career as a salesperson, I worked in a car dealership (surprise!). And, as is usually the case with car dealerships, there was a string of them down our main road—different names and titles, all down a main strip in between towns. This always makes for an odd tension and introduces an extra edge of competition. It's easier to feel driven to beat the other guys when you can see them a hundred yards away, like huge modern castles housing old blood rivals, their salespeople quietly plotting your dealership's eventual downfall.

Seeing your competition just down the street is infinitely more motivating than having them across a dense city or even small town. When you're mid-downtown without anyone else in near view, it's hard to muster any kind of school spirit. You hear vague reports about the sorts of numbers the Other Place is doing, and you compare how many cars they're putting out on average, but these are more like the stuff of distant legends and indigenous folklore than a comparative summary or something to set your watch by.

When I would take customers out on a test drive, they would often ask me questions. Now, I will touch more heavily on this in the Product Knowledge section, but here's a sneaky strategy I devised: if a person was asking an unusual number of questions during a test drive, I would ask him or her which other cars they were looking at, specifically those at other dealerships. After a moment's hesitation, they would usually tell me which rival cars had caught their eye. I would actually bring the car into my competitor's lot and put our model right next to the vehicle that was contending for my customer's money. I'd explain to the customer why the car he or she had been driving was better, and not only that, but I'd point out some of the advantages of the other's.

I would go over the look of the car I was selling, the engine, the safety features, the interior, the options available—everything I knew I would toss out to the customer to convince them to buy. But not only that, I'd point out the benefits inherent in the *other* car. Many of them would interrupt me partway through to ask, "Gord—why are you doing this?" The reason is simple.

> Just because your employers are allowing you the privilege of making money through their business, this doesn't mean that you owe them anything.

I would tell them, "Mr. or Mrs. Customer, while I do like working here, I have no idea where I'm going to be next month. Maybe I'll be working here, or maybe another dealership will give me a better offer and I'll move there. The important thing is that you get what you're looking for, and all this looks completely different on paper than it does in real life." And, of course, there's always the possibility of in-house leasing.

The fact is, just because your employers are allowing you the privilege of making money through their business, this doesn't mean that you owe them anything. When you really think about it, you have signed a contract with your establishment, whatever it may be,

> This is your living. This is your career. This is how you pay your bills, feed your children, and exist in society.

that for X number of work hours and sales you put through, they will pay you Y percent/dollars. You might like the people, you might like the money, and you might be grateful for the opportunity, but you have to remember that at the end of the day you're breaking even with them. You're holding up your end by selling; they're holding up their end by paying you (I hope). It's an equal transaction, keeping both of you in the "plus" column indefinitely. Never forget that if they could sell product more easily and directly via charming, well-to-do robots, and obliterate your position altogether, they would do it in an instant. You wouldn't even have time to pack—you could just show up to work one day and find your things on the lawn.

That's the nature of business, and you have to be shrewd. If you get an excellent offer, consider it carefully, but don't let loyalty get in the way of it. This is your living. This is your *career*. This is how you pay your bills, feed your children, and exist in society. Don't let emotion entangle you in your end of the bargain, because if that Bad Day ever came and machines really did rule the industry, emotion certainly wouldn't tangle up their end. No sir, not likely—and you'd be very lucky indeed to get an unemployment cheque within a month or so of application in this country.

DEAL CONTROL

The smartest thing you can do is make customers feel at home and in charge. It sounds funny, but the more in control customers feel, the easier it is to direct and guide them in the direction you want them to go. It all comes down to stimulus and alertness. If people feel controlled and helpless, they will become hyper-aware and automatically defensive. They'll close down and refuse to commit to anything. Feelings of subjection and vulnerability are negative stimuli; they are not conducive to making a sale, let alone a deal you can both feel good about. You want positive stimulation. You want to offer your customers camaraderie, humour, comfort, reassurance—*control.*

> The smartest thing you can do is make customers feel at home and in charge.

From the moment they walk in the front door, when you approach and shake hands, saying all the right things and hitting all the proper cues, you are convincing them that they are unique, critical to your existence, and utterly in control. Over time, you will learn to polish exactly what to say and in which order, given the circumstance(s). Before long, you will go from shivering red fox in the tundra to well-camouflaged timber wolf lurking through Arctic plains. Very few things are cooler than polar bears, for obvious reasons, and after you've run the course a time or two you will be just as skilful and confident as those godless beasts.

That's why, when you take your customers out on a test drive, you go a specific, preplanned route. You tell them when to turn ("Hang a left up here, if you will"), and you suggestively talk about how much torque and horsepower this particular car has on long (and remarkably unpoliced) stretches of road. Accentuate the turning radius and quick responsiveness in tight spaces you just "happen" to be in, or the sensitive brakes in places where the road might end suddenly. Take a turn driving, finish it up for them and do everything they didn't get a chance to do (whether or not this was due to clever planning).

Never, never talk numbers during a test drive. Customers will want to chat during the test drive. Keep them occupied—talk about the weather if you have to. Keep the conversation relevant, professional, and vehicle centred.

And most importantly of all, make sure you park the car for them in the lot. There's nothing to take the flow out of a test drive like sitting in the car with customers for five minutes while they struggle to make a death blow at the parallel park (or even straight pull-in, you'll find). Before long, you will want to offer to park it *for* them, but if drivers leave the situation defeated, it will be very difficult to make them feel excited or encouraged about the buy. That brief encounter becomes eternal very quickly, and neither one of you will want to look the other in the eye afterward. While all the information

> **Never talk numbers during a test drive and when the drive is done be sure to park the car for them.**

you'll find in this book is extremely important, I would stress the gargantuan nature of this point. Your job can be a lot easier if you do yourself favours like this one, and there is nothing as basic or easy as simple acts of mercy. If you can remove the awkwardness and painful drag, you are proving to everybody (including yourself) that you've really mastered the art of the deal, and key selling strategies are most definitely a part of *that*.

CHAPTER TWO

CLOSING

Closing is (arguably) the most important stage in the sales process. It is your Grail, your target, the meaning of your quest. It is the undertaking that you strive for. I will illustrate for you now in a simple, easy-to-follow Question & Answer format, the significance of the aforementioned skill:

Q: What is a sale without a close?

A: *Non-existent.*

The close is your ending, the step that actually solidifies the sale. It is your goal, your Act Three. It is where and when

> Closing is the most important stage in the sales process. The close is your ending, the step that actually solidifies the sale.

you push your customer over the edge of consideration and into action. Any great talker can sit in a rut for months if he doesn't know how to close. However, I should clarify that in the business of sales this particular circumstance is not referred to as a rut—it is more commonly known (in the Professional Sales World) as a *lack of skill*.

I once watched an orientation video featuring the great story *Glengarry Glen Ross*, in which they outlined their foolproof tactic for directing a sale as follows: **ABC**

Or, in more detail,

Always Be Closing

This is wrong.

If you are always closing, *you are not listening*. Closing is an end-stage proposition, not a state of mind you can expect to carry you throughout. It is a place you want to arrive at, not a country whose flag you secretly harbour at all times. Trying to end a sale at every juncture is rude and transparent, and your customers will not only quickly realize your plan of attack, but they will be offended by your lack of interest in their needs.

> If you are always closing, you are not listening

However, it's the right idea. They even got honourable mention in the movie *Jerry Maguire*. Their idea is based around always driving toward the end, and that could not be more accurate.

You must think of a sale (and especially the close) as a bicycle. The rear wheel is the salesperson. It is the all-powerful "creator of velocity", from which all sales and income effuse. It discharges money and prestige and *traffic*. Simply put, the bike doesn't roll without this driving force.

This brings us to the front wheel, which would be the customer. He will roll if you push him correctly. He is there to be directed; his very function is to be propelled by the back wheel. The front wheel believes itself to be in control, because it decides which direction to take—what to buy, for example, and for how much. But the back wheel can and does guide it—this is *your* job.

You should think of the tools in this book as your pedals. If the bike flows seamlessly, and each part does its duty correctly, there is very little evidence of where (or even if) the accelerating force originates, and centrifugal force is assumed. This is also true with a sale; allowing the customer to believe that he is in control, while silently directing his motion, is the higher plane you are striving for. Once you can do that effectively, you will find the things you want shockingly close at hand.

> As soon as your customer steps out of your sight, the likelihood of a sale declines dramatically.

I had a reputation for being one of the fastest closers in the business—within twenty to thirty minutes of shaking the customer's hand, I could have a sale under my belt. I had very few "comeback" customers, of course referring to customers who decided to leave my presence to make a decision. As soon as your customer steps out of your sight, the likelihood of a sale declines dramatically.

The customer is leaving, we must assume, to compare your price to another. We must assume that he is going to take your price to a competitor, and we must assume that your competitor will try to beat it. Do you see the downward spiral? It's a very basic, very common confluence of events. Very soon after these things have happened, you will find yourself light one customer or battling with another dealership, wasting your time for a theoretical sale that may or may not happen. And even then, you're into a lower profit margin, and I don't know about you, but I've never been interested in lower profit margins. I'm here to make money. You should be, too. Keep the customer there and interested. How do you accomplish this, you wonder.

As King George III once said to the Archbishop of Canterbury,

"Come, my Lord Bishop, I will show you the way to heaven."

Could you
Would you
Ain't you gonna
If I asked you
Would you wanna.

Memorize that. Write that down. It's like poetry, or it might as well be. Haiku poet Basho doesn't have *anything* on the (soon-to-be) award-winning CY-WYAYGIFIAYWYW technique. Those are the five questions that you need to remember for a close. This is how you win a sale, boys and girls.

Could you, would you, ain't you gonna, if I asked you, would you wanna.

Say that ten times out loud. Don't think! Just do it!

Could you, would you, ain't you gonna, if I asked you, would you wanna.
Could you, would you, ain't you gonna, if I asked you, would you wanna.
Could you, would you, ain't you gonna, if I asked you, would you wanna.
Could you, would you, ain't you gonna, if I asked you, would you wanna.
Could you, would you, ain't you gonna, if I asked you, would you wanna.

(Chorus x2)

Could you, would you, ain't you gonna, if I asked you, would you wanna.
Could you, would you, ain't you gonna, if I asked you, would you wanna.
Could you, would you, ain't you gonna, if I asked you, would you wanna.
Could you, would you, ain't you gonna, if I asked you, would you wanna.
Could you, would you, ain't you gonna, if I asked you, would you wanna!

COULD YOU:

"Mr./Ms. Customer, could you buy this vehicle today if the numbers were right?"

Find out if they have the finances to do what you want them to do. Are they in a position to buy? Or are they really just browsing? That's a very key piece of advice to have. If they have three other dealerships lined up to visit that day, then you need to find out—fast—so you know what kind of self-imposed deadline they're on. Also, do they have the garage space? Do they plan on trading in their existing car? Could they put the money down and commit, today, if they wanted to? If the answer is yes, then a lot of the work is really done for you.

WOULD YOU:

"Mr./Ms. Customer, would you buy this product today?"

Is it feasibly something they're interested in doing? Is the interior everything they'd want it to be? Does it have the level of performance they're looking for? This is when you find out the specifics. Would they, at this price, buy this model of car? If not, there are things you can do to customize the product—as well as beef up the price. There is very big money in the little conveniences. This is a very good thing to be an expert on. Usually you have to wait a few months for the after-market to catch up, but if you can get yourself in close contact with a few customization outlets and shops, anything you can't do at the dealership they can likely do there. If the customers don't like the paint job, or maybe saw something on television that intrigued them, it's easy to impress them that you've done your homework as far as what's out there.

AREN'T YOU GONNA:

"Mr./Ms. Customer, aren't you going to buy it today?"

Be direct! Ask for the business! People hate saying no! What's the worst that can happen—they say no? So what! Ask why not!

In all seriousness, ask them why not, and then sit back and listen. Really listen. The first person to speak loses. Let them tell you why.

A very common answer is, "My spouse isn't here." Well, when can they be here? You're either closing to an appointment

> Be direct! Ask for the business! People hate saying no!

(which is acceptable) or finding out what the real objections are. If they're not sure or can't give you a date, then you reply,

"Well, give me just a moment to speak with my manager, and we can go and see her."

Very few people will object to that. Why would they? They are thinking, *I honestly get to drive this shiny new car across town and surprise my spouse at work? What a nice little treat!* It doesn't *cost* them anything, after all. Just ask to get their information down on paper. What do they have to lose?

You're creating a process of visualization with the customer now. They're imagining themselves owning this car and making this drive on their own. It's very easy to get used to the idea of a new vehicle, and suddenly all the things they don't like about it are starting to fade. They're thinking of it as a *possession* now, not an abstract idea of a possibility. Generally speaking, if a man drives a new car to his wife's work to show it to her, that surprised wife is going to assume her husband feels strongly about it, and vice versa.

> **Always try to seek out objections.**

You should always try to seek out objections. If people have objections they don't want to voice, you absolutely cannot use that. All it can do is hurt you. People don't like to be bullied. They like to be asked for their opinions and then have their fears laid to rest— whatever that means for your situation. You need all the information you can get to close the deal, because the more you know about their frame of mind, the more power you have to direct it.

IF I ASKED YOU:

"Mr./Ms. Customer, if I asked you, would you buy this car?"

Keep asking for the business! What are we *really* talking about here? Once you have somebody in that frame of mind, you've made progress. Unless they're considering it, it's not going to happen. Plant the seed! Walk them through it! It's such a simple and straightforward way to sell, and 99 per cent of all salespeople completely overlook it! Don't just try to schmooze your way through every deal—be honest, and encourage them to be honest!

They will respect you and feel respected. They will grin while shaking your hand and ask to see you specifically when they come back. They will mention to their friends over lunch the way they didn't feel forced or coerced. This is how you establish repeat customers. They need to feel comfortable and in control. Once you've got them seriously considering the sale as an option, it's not a far leap into action. This is the evolution of sales. This is today's market. This is how you impress people.

WOULD YOU WANNA:

"Mr./Ms. Customer, would you want to buy this product today?"

As a salesperson, it is absolutely your job to find the right item. Are you demonstrating the right product? Just because they picked a specific one doesn't mean that it's necessarily the right one— and it's up to you to figure that out, too. If the answer turns out to be no, the customers haven't

> As a salesperson, it is absolutely your job to find the right item.

been wasting your time with the wrong product, *you've* been wasting *theirs* by making assumptions instead of asking questions. Are you selling them the right vehicle? If not, find a new one! There is nothing wrong with bringing up people's true negative feelings about a sale. It's better if you don't just gloss them over. If you take the time to assess their actual ideas, opinions, and needs, you might find they're better suited for another car. Your customers are relieved, because they don't feel backed into a corner and are now in a position to walk away with a (potentially) better deal than what they came for.

What did we say about the front wheel of a bicycle? *Let them think they're in control.* That's what this section is all about. If you can remember the five questions, you won't have a problem with closing. Keep them close and always be conscious of them; treat them the way that cowboys treat their six-shooters. The five questions are always applicable, and they are always important. You cannot expect to just breeze through a sale without any application of strategy or tact. Use these things the way a carpenter uses his tools—a big, flat piece of lumber can't grow up into a door on its own.

> The five questions are always applicable, and they are always important.

Your company will present you with tools similar to these. Use those, too. These companies spend thousands (sometimes millions) of dollars on creating strategies that work and then refining them into a process that's useful to everyone. They boil it all down to bite-size information that anybody could understand, and it always plays off basic human psyche and instinct. They want you to make them money, make no mistake about that, and the best way to generate income through employees is to make sure they're doing their job correctly and consistently. Use your resources! Likely, by this point in the book you're beginning to see the real differences between serious, professional salespeople and everyone else.

> They want you to make them money, make no mistake about that.

CHAPTER THREE

UNIQUE MARKETS

In any sales area, you will always be encouraged by the administration to explore niche or unique markets. If you're in the furniture business, or realty, or any respectable business at all, they will guide you in that direction. However, most sales representatives shy away from the ambiguity of that; the very prospect of customers outside their normal walk-in traffic looms dangerously in the distance as unknown and worrisome. It is the "other kind" of sales. It is "out of the way" and must be hunted down, and thus it is unworthy. "Why, there are avenues set up for this sort of thing! Specialists! That's not my area! If they want my services, they know where to find me!"

> Many sales reps make the mistake of thinking "If they want my services, they know where to find me!"

At any dealership, at any time of the year, there is a collection of salty old dogs that I have come to call "coffee groups". What that boils down to, so to speak, is a handful of sales reps that clump together regularly and discuss how slow business is. They sip coffee and sagely complain about the door traffic and how things didn't used to be this way. They guffaw and mutter and spew angry talk about their customers and how much more money they think they *should* be making. I never wound up in these places, save one or two shameful days before I realized where I was and what we were doing. That's not just because I don't drink coffee, as they do tend to sell juice and pop in such establishments. No, the reason I never found myself in those places is because *I didn't have time*. I was too busy selling, even in the "darker months".

I had people coming in from the Harley Owners Group. I had families of people with disabilities coming in. I was a race car driver before I was a salesman, so I knew which types of trucks the race car drivers would need to pull their cars to the track. I specialized in trucks, actually. Auto Trader advertised that I was the truck specialist for my dealerships. If you're living up to your potential, you won't have time to get caught up in all that "doom and gloom". I call it "recession proofing"—insulating your career with constant money-makers to generate sales for yourself, enough so that your dealership could burn down, and you'd still be meeting your quota and even exceeding it via phone calls and personal meetings.

> Becoming a specialist is simply a way of recession proofing your career.

I took my job one step further. I was always the top sales representative for my dealership, even in the beginning, much to the surprise and grief of my colleagues. That doesn't just *happen*, my friends, as opportunity doesn't typically knock quite as often as our elders seem to remember. If you really want to make a splash, you have to have a standby method of generating your *own* sales. That is where your ingenuity and genius come in. You have it, of course, as we both well know—it just needs harnessing. Let me show you how that developed for me.

> If you really want to make a splash... have a standby method of generating your own sales.

I have always been involved in my community. At eighteen, I was fervently seeking ways to better the people around me, and I decided to help out with the Easter Seals foundation. It's a wonderful assortment of dedicated individuals who provide assistance to disabled children. I met the district coordinator at a meeting, and after brief and skilful conversation, she asked if I'd be interested in becoming more involved. As a result of these meetings, I became the first district chair for Peterborough, and few things in my life have been so rewarding.

I never used charity for networking, and I've never sold a car to somebody I was directly involved with through Easter Seals. I was always very conscious of how that could complicate my life and my involvement with the kids. It's not ethical to use charity to sell anything, let's make that clear right from the get-go. My interest with the Easter Seals society or any similar foundation begins and ends with helping people, and in those arenas, my accomplishments speak for themselves.

We would go on weekend retreats, have conferences that lasted days—it generally involved a lot of time and travel. They offered great workshops. At one workshop, I spent a day in a wheelchair, just to get a better idea of what that confinement would be like. They had me wear mittens for a long period, so I was unable to use my fingers or manipulate my digits the way I normally could. It really opened my eyes and gave me a new perspective on physical challenges. You don't know what pedestrian difficulty is until you've tried to see a movie in a chair—and that's just the beginning.

> Once I became the specialist, the management and other salespeople actually referred customers to me, and for good reason.

These new perspectives on disability and restriction got me thinking. Once I'd had a (small) taste of the sort of things some of these kids go through daily, my mind started to wander in the direction of business. I was selling cars for a living at that point, and I started to look into what sort of attachments and modifications they required to accommodate different challenges.

I'm sure you can imagine where I went with that. Before long, I was the AutoAbility specialist for my dealership. If you had to buy a vehicle for a person with a disability, I was the guy you talked to. The management and other salespeople actually referred customers to me, and for good reason. It's not an easy process to upgrade a van to optimum wheelchair accessibility.

The vehicle would have to be loaded onto a train and shipped from Toronto to Arizona, converted, and sent back eight to ten weeks later. This usually cost between $100,000 and $120,000 in the end. It started slow, but before long I'd have two in transit while I sold two more at any given time. I was running a firm pace of five to six sales every month before I left that particular dealership. We even had systems in place to help them afford it, and we used the factory and Easter Seals to help us come up with payment plans for the parents.

It was really an amazing thing to be a part of. Usually you don't sell cars to feel good about yourself. You do it for money, not to generate a feeling of contribution and self-worth—but I really felt as if I were a part of something, even if I was making money doing it. A lot of people gave me sideways glances over that whole process, but there's nothing wrong with having a customer base of challenged families. Ayn Rand wrote a tremendous book called *The Virtue of Selfishness* that I'd recommend to any salesperson. The title is a little intimidating, but it calls into question the way society looks down its collective nose at people who generate money for themselves.

Observe the indecency of what passes for moral judgments today. An industrialist who produces a fortune, and a gangster who robs a bank are regarded as equally immoral, since they both sought wealth for their own "selfish" benefit. A young man who gives up his career in order to support his parents and never rises beyond the rank of grocery clerk is regarded as morally superior to the

young man who endures an excruciating struggle and achieves his
personal ambition.
—*Ayn Rand*

But we're getting off topic. To bring this back to the subject at hand, there is nothing wrong with generating money from such processes *as long as no person or group of persons are wronged or taken advantage of.* Nobody lost out in my process except the other sales representatives, but it's up to those people to come up with their own niche markets (this is, after all, a competitive field). I helped open doors for disadvantaged people, not close them. I'm sorry if this sounds like an excessive amount of justification, but I just don't want to lose you. We'll talk more about ethics in my Professionalism chapter.

> **Nobody lost out in my process except the other sales representatives.**

So, let me make it clear that this is not for everybody. I had an interest and a background, and I stumbled into something I was comfortable with and had deep knowledge about. I'm not telling you to seek out charities and pounce on them like brutal dogs, and I'm not saying that every town has a children's organization that could be a potential money train for you. What I am saying, however, is that your success in niche markets is limited by your own ingenuity *only*.

There are a great many things you can do to generate your own unique market or money flow. I could write an entire second book about that, but let me quickly give you an example of one thing that was extremely successful for me.

There is always a pile of product brochures lying around any sales office, car or otherwise. I found myself a company letterhead with my dealership's name on the top of it, and using Microsoft Word, I typed my name at the bottom—along with Special Employee Purchase Offer. Whatever the company's name

> Your success in niche markets is limited by your own ingenuity only.

was, I fired it in and made copies. Whatever our current promotion was, be it 0% financing, low lease rates, etc., I very carefully cut out a picture that was appropriate for whatever I was trying to sell and take it to a copying business. I made colour copies and showed them to my manager. They looked like professionally printed product brochures, and with permission from the appropriate people, I took a day and went around to all the big local businesses—mostly manufacturing companies and things like that, all big corporate businesses. And I took along gift baskets.

This is where your God-given gift of gab shines through, as does influence, which you should at all times wield like a broadsword. You can get a gift basket made for fifteen to twenty dollars. Mine were filled with things like coffees, biscuits, teas, chocolates, cookies, things of that nature. These gift baskets, along with about fifty carefully doctored brochures, made their way into the hands of the receptionists of all these local big businesses. Even if there were signs up that discouraged solicitors, I walked up to the front desks and asked the people working there if they might help me. I introduced myself (very politely), displayed the brochures first, and then insisted that no matter what they do with that pile of paper, they themselves take the gift baskets as a personal token of gratitude. I asked them to please put these in a stack by the coffee maker, on bulletin boards, in mailboxes, what have you—and I would tell that person that their company had been selected by *my* company for reduced pricing and special deals. These deals, however, were perhaps more common than I might have let on, but as they say: "Deals is deals".

Let's say you tried this, and it failed astronomically. Let's say that all those copies and gift baskets only generated one sale. Guess what, friend? That one sale just paid for all your baskets, your copies, and your effort. And that's not to mention repeat business from that one person, plus referrals. You might have just won yourself a lifetime customer. And if you play it the way I did, you might win yourself *many* lifetime customers. How impressed do you figure your managers will be with that kind of initiative? I can dimly recall streamers and confetti from the management branch when I presented them with my idea.

> The key to unique markets has nothing to do with what is currently selling at your outlet and everything to do with your own expertise.

And that's the key to unique markets, my dear friends. It has nothing to do with what is currently selling at your outlet and everything to do with your own expertise. This is where *you* shine. This is your chance to take the thing *you* are best at (selling) and meld it with something you hold close.

We are all daily faced with difficult decisions; chief among them is whether to fulfil responsibility or achieve what we commonly know as "fun". If you can balance yourself correctly, you will be amazed at how often these two things, i.e., your recreational activity and

> The things you do on your own initiative for joy can often spill over into what you do out of necessity for money.

your business life, can overlap. You can absolutely meld the two into one cohesive ball of awesome—but if and how you do that is entirely up to you. I'm not suggesting that every single person alive should do charity work and also sell cars, but I am suggesting that the things you do on your own initiative for joy can often spill over into what you do out of necessity for money.

Let's say, for example, that you're a camper. You like to camp, and thus, camping is what you do. Who's to say that this can't be an integral part of your work life? What attachments do you use on your vehicle? What special parts are you looking at? What's your personal average baggage load? How could you account for varying loads and build that into a vehicle package? Go to outdoorsmen shows and hunting/fishing shops and drop off cards and fliers to generate interest in this vehicle package. If at every camping store that particular group of people go to they find your face and phone number, then you're going to get more calls—I don't care who you are. That's how advertising works.

Think about it. You could be the on-site camping guy, the one that customers hear about from their friends and look to for advice on how they should be rigging their getups in order to, indeed, *get up and go.* If you come at it right, you could create *lore* about yourself. When you go camping, do you use a trailer? To pull a trailer, you need a special vehicle. You need the right size truck, with the right GVW rating, engine, transmission, etc. Is it a diesel? A four-wheel drive? That's a market, friends.

This opens interesting opportunities in the direction of justification for *amalgamation,* meaning, of course, that you can spend ridiculous amounts of money on unique outdoors equipment for personal use. How can you feel guilty for that? You're not just doing something for yourself; it's for your *customers,* too. You need to know what you're selling. It's an *investment,* and a potentially high-yielding investment at that!

> Your favourite pastime is a ready-made sales market.

Are you a hockey mom or a hockey dad? Likely you've already done the research into minivans, their APEAL (Automotive Performance, Execution, and Layout) ratings, their safety and luxury ratings, the best navigational systems for that particular van, rear-seat entertainment systems, and so on. You can relate to those customers, because you *are one of them.* That's a market.

Maybe you're a volunteer firefighter. Maybe you have a passion for collector or performance cars. Go to car shows and get some phone numbers—you can create your own car show! It's not that difficult. Get permission from management, and bring out some guys with old vintage cars to do a Show and Shine at your dealership. Those guys love putting their cars on display, and people love seeing them. Wheel out a souped-up truck and some flashy speeders; put out balloons, business cards, fliers, and brochures; set up a booth, and talk to people as they come through—you'd be amazed at how many people will show up! Put the bug in their ear!

> No matter who you are, you have a built-in natural market that you can tap into.

No matter who you are, you have a built-in natural market that you can tap into. You just need to use it. Door traffic can be slow. Get inventive. What do *you* have? Why do you have that attachment you have? What aftermarket merchandise have you bought?

What are your interests? What are your hobbies? Go and get a pen right now, and make a list in this book, point form.

1.
2.
3.
4.
5.
6.
7.
8.
9.
10.

Take those points of interest and ask yourself: Who do I know that can help me turn this into a money-maker?

This is why I'm so baffled at people who don't seem absolutely beside themselves with enthusiasm about sales. You can take things virtually anywhere you want them to go. You need to pay your dues and prove yourself as a salesperson, work the kinks out, and once you have a name for yourself, you can go anywhere and do anything. It's not hard numbers and raw labour; it's *people*, essentially. You deal in free will and traffic influence. It's a God-given gift that you can harness into your dream job. People are fluid, and so, then, is sales.

> People are fluid, and so, then, is sales.

Everything is disposable, and everything is flexible. All you need is drive. The rest will just come.

CHAPTER FOUR

PROFESSIONALISM

I believe that professionalism is extremely important. For proof of that, please mark your place in this book now, close it, and examine the cover. If you've followed these directions carefully, you will find the root word of this chapter's title *in the title of the book*. Many sales reps will often stray from this out of overconfidence, ineptitude, or just plain laziness—and that includes the seasoned veterans. Men and women with a great deal of experience and success can cap their own monthly sales by ignoring the fundamentals of professionalism. It's an easy thing to overlook, especially if you've allowed confidence to override good sense. Professionalism is, in short, your immediate credibility. It is your presentation of worth to your customers. It is the quickest and easiest way to prove to anybody you deal with that you are good at your job and that they should be dealing with you professionally and consistently.

> Professionalism is, in short, your immediate credibility.

There are many ways to lose a customer, and if you ignore this section of the book as something even monkeys know, you will experience a great deal of them first-hand.

PROFESSIONAL PERSUASIVENESS

There is no worse opening than "Hello. Can I help you?" That, dear friends, is an closed-ended question, and we try to avoid those in our initial greetings. Potential clients could say no, and at that juncture it would be rude to pursue the sale.

"Hello, and welcome to ABC motors. My name is Gordon O'Neill, and I am your professional sales consultant/new sales and leasing consultant. And your name is?" You say this while you're shaking hands. They will tell you their name, because it costs them nothing, and you're holding their hand. They know that you're not going to let go until they've responded. And they will.

"My name is Gertrude."

"It's a pleasure to meet you, Gertrude. How may I assist your buying process today?"

They might respond:

"Well, I'm just looking."
"Well, I'm interesting in buying a van."
"I'm interested in a truck."
"I wanna buy a sedan."

Whatever the case may be, they've opened a window for you. You can help them now. Hooray! If they tell you they're just interested in a brochure, excellent.

"What is the vehicle you're interested in today?" Don't just give them a brochure with your business card stapled to it, because in all likelihood they're going to leave after that. Ask if they want to test drive that car, and ask if they'll allow you to do a full price presentation for them. It's great if they just take a brochure, but offer to make sure that the car is suitable for them. Tell them it'll just take a moment, and you'll be able to answer any questions they might have.

"I have all the vehicles on the lot, Gertrude, and they're ready for immediate test drive." Then you can walk them through your meet and greet, qualify, price proposal, and assumptive close.

My wife always jokes with me that I don't know how to relax. What she means by that is I'm always polite with people, I'm always well dressed, and I like to take care of myself. I believe that you should always conduct yourself in a way that is pleasant and kind. After my shift is over, I carry my professionalism with me everywhere I go. I always look presentable, or I don't leave the house. Even when I'm out riding my Harley, I still have nice pants on and a button-down shirt. I don't wear ripped jeans or paint-stained shirts, because you never know when you're going to meet your next client.

> I carry my professionalism with me everywhere I go.

As a financial securities advisor, I used to deal with mutual funds and RRSPs, life insurance, investment products, wealth management, etc. One night at about eight-thirty, just before a local stationary store was going to close, I ran out at the last minute to pick up some office supplies. I just happened to run across somebody that worked in the establishment. We started talking and joking, had a short conversation about the store, and next thing you know we got onto the topic of the new baby he and his wife had. I explained what I did for a living, and he expressed interest in updating their life insurance policies. I gave him my business card (as a professional, you should always have some with you) and didn't pursue it any further. A week later they called back, and I wound up selling them both life insurance.

> No matter where you are and what you're doing, you're on the clock. That's how commission works.

It just goes to show that, no matter where you are and what you're doing, you're on the clock. That's how commission works. You will get whatever money you *earn*, and not a penny more or less. That's what keeps smart salespeople out of coffee clubs. I can guarantee you that those guys aren't going to pay your mortgage. They don't need a car; they drove a car to work. Oftentimes they have company cars. Instead of spending that half-hour in a coffee club, spend twenty minutes doing some product knowledge. When little Timmy needs braces, you're not going to turn to your colleagues—excuse me, your *competition*—for a sale. You're going to turn to the customer. Spend that time honing your skills, and always keep in mind that the next person you meet could be your next customer.

If I had been standing there in ripped jeans and a T-shirt, do you honestly think he would have looked at me as a viable resource for planning his future? Would he have laughed me off and maybe taken my card? Or would he have talked to me at all? It's sad to say, but some people just won't respond to others who seem to be in a lower class than they are. You need to keep things like that in mind and even play off them if you expect to make serious money in this arena.

ATTIRE

Call me old-fashioned, but I believe that in a business setting men should wear the traditional suit jackets and ties, and women should wear nice business suits. This is not because I am a patriarchal, closed-minded oppressor; this is because it's what I've learned people expect. It calms them. It soothes them. It puts them at ease. Make no mistake: no matter what your gender, religion, race, or orientation, as a salesperson you are absolutely in the business of calming and soothing your customers. You want them feeling relaxed and happy, not out of their element and cautious. You're impressing on your customers that you are worthwhile.

> Studies have shown that within the first sixty seconds of meeting you, customers know whether or not they're going to do business with you.

I use this as a guide:
Look good, feel good.
Feel good, play good.
Play good, pay good.

You want to make sure you look good; you want to play hard as a stress relief—and when you feel good and you play good, then the pay is good. You're healthy, you're happy, and you're confident. You're the person I want handling my sale.

Studies have shown that within the first sixty seconds of meeting you, customers know whether or not they're going to do business with you. People are going to look at your shoes, your jewellery, and your suit to judge whether or not you're right for them—and make no mistake, they will be judging.

If you live in a climate where there's snow, have an outside and an inside pair of shoes. Keep liquid polish inside your desk. It's important to keep some cheap shoe polish around, because it dries quickly and it's great to touch up scuffs on your shoes. It's also important to keep an extra suit around—that's right, an alternate outfit. What if you get splashed by a car driving through a puddle? You don't want to have to go home to change, especially if you commute. That's a great way to lose out on a lot of money if it's a busy day. If you have a locker, that's perfect. If not, there's no reason why you can't have a

> People are going to look at you ... and make no mistake, they will be judging.

change of clothes in your car, and for me that included a couple of different shirts. You just never know.

If you're going to be dealing with customers from a broad spectrum, it's important to refrain from wearing expensive jewellery. Perceived value is something—by all means, wear your jewellery for high-earning customers at a top-end dealership. But if you're working at a used-car dealership, nobody wants to buy a ten-thousand-dollar car from a person wearing a ten-thousand-dollar watch. I know it's unfortunate, and we all like to wear nice things, but you have to be sure not to intimidate or offend your customers.

I like watches. I actually collect fine pens, as well. I have several Montblanc pens, worth upwards of two thousand dollars. When I make a big sale, I like to treat myself to something expensive. I have a Gucci, a Rolex, a Breitling, an Oris, a Raymond Weil … My goal is to someday have a twenty-thousand-dollar pen, because

> It is so important to stay in the mindset of a winner. You need the power of positive thinking.

the day that I can justify that purchase is the day I know everything else is in place.

It is so important to treat yourself and stay in the mindset of a winner. You need the power of positive thinking. Don't let yourself get lost in the business. If you falter from that mindset, you'll show it in your sales. Be a winner, but stay professional. Not everybody wants to see your success; some will take it as flaunting.

WORK SPACE

This is your office, desk, what have you—the area where you conduct your business and see your clients. Although this is where you spend the majority of your day, you shouldn't think of this as your own private place. You should think of this as a tool. It's yet another weapon in your ever-expanding arsenal. This is not *your* desk; this is your representation of your worth as a business associate to the customer. You should spend the extra money for desk accessories and brand-name supplies. Don't go overboard, but everything should be neat, it should match, and it should work. People are simple creatures, and they're impressed by pretty things. Labels, Post-its, organizers, Rolodexes, a sleek laptop or fixed computer, binders and binder holders, laminated pages—all that really nice stuff you might not even actually need or use adds visual credibility during a first impression.

> This is not *your* desk; this is your representation of your worth as a business associate to the customer.

It doesn't matter what field you're in. You want to make sure those people will feel comfortable and secure in your environment. You're asking them for their driver's licences, their social insurance numbers, and other very personal information. I don't need to go into detail as to how these things relate.

Another item is coffee. I don't drink coffee, but 90 per cent of the population does. There's nothing messier. Coffee spills, it stains, and when that mug is empty it's an eyesore. It's a good idea to keep your coffee mug in your top desk drawer so that it's out of the way and out of everyone's mind. Same thing with pop cans and bottles.

There should not be food present on the desk in any work environment. That makes the customer feel unimportant and intrusive, as if he or she is distracting you from your own personal care. I don't care if it's five minutes from closing time. That customer needs to feel that he is the most important thing happening in your work space at that time, and you should never allow yourself to seem distracted by inanimate objects. Your desk is your sales temple. It is your altar built to and for the customer. You rule it; it does not rule you, and every-

> Your desk is your sales temple. It is your altar built to and for the customer. Everything on it is geared toward your customer.

thing on it is geared toward your customer. You should appear mechanical and fluid. Your break comes when nobody is around and you have nobody to impress (or leave unimpressed).

It's a good idea to eat in your staff lunchroom, or even your car, if you have to. I used to, and I'm better for it. Unless you have a little DustBuster screwed into the inside of your desk and are willing to vacuum after every meal, it's a bad call to bring food near your work area.

After eating, go to the washroom and make sure you've got no food between your teeth, in your beard or moustache, on your tie, etc. Keep away from garlic and onions, things that are going to hurt your breath. Restrict your diet at work to inoffensive-smelling foods. I like to keep mouthwash and a toothbrush on hand. I've met many people who like to use gum to remedy bad breath, but many of us find it difficult to be inconspicuous while chewing gum. It's a loud, unattractive process, and you really don't need it. It's the same thing with candy. However, I would encourage you to keep a full candy dish at the edge of your desk, facing your customer. If you can't resist eating the candy yourself, then I'd say you're best to leave it aside entirely.

HYGIENE

I cannot stress to you how important odour control is. I understand that you may have conditions or health complications, and that is absolutely understandable. You can actually work around that. As a matter of fact, odours can be good and bad. It might seem to strike you that I don't know what I'm talking about, but I'll ask you to refer to everything I've said previously for credit—or even collateral—just until we can get through this part. Stand by me, friends, and give trust.

If it is a hot day, and you are sweating, customers are not going to want to stand near you. Conversely, you may be wearing an excessive amount of cologne or body spray, which could also set the customer off. Some people are allergic to certain perfumes or colognes, and if you wear too much you can cause a reaction in your customer.

Smoking is usually not permitted inside car dealerships, but you can often find smoking areas in bigger dealerships. A lot of salespeople smoke, especially in the car industry, and a lot of representatives will go outside for a cigarette when things are slow. They'll wander the lots and look at cars, often in view of the customers. Again, this is wrong, and it's careless. This isn't an image that you want to portray—never mind the smell. Even smokers will remark that they don't like it when people smell like cigarettes. Many people are offended even by the sight of smoking, as they may have family members that have passed away as the result of lung cancer. When you're in sales, you represent your place of business. This is common sense. You're the one being the professional. This is your workplace, not theirs.

> When you're in sales, you represent your place of business.

Shave every day. It's not hard, it takes about two minutes, and it will drastically improve your credibility. I've had to shave every day since I was fourteen, because the men in my family tend to mature young and remain manly throughout the rest of their lives. This is another challenge I've been faced with, but I continue to overcome that obstacle, as I expect you would. If you have thick hair, shower first or during to soften the strain on your skin. Always shave with hot water, and shave with the grain to avoid ingrown hair. I know it sounds ludicrous to give advice on shaving, but it's amazing how often you see people in this business that have absolutely no idea how to care for themselves.

Even if you can skip a day without shaving, don't. Five o'clock shadows look sloppy.

> There are a million different ways to be professional and achieve worth in your potential clients' eyes.

There are a million different ways to be professional and achieve worth in your potential clients' eyes through a very short encounter. I hope that you take these ideas to heart and use them in your everyday endeavours, as well as use that template to generate your own ideas. Every work space is different. Always keep in mind what people expect to see and what you have to offer, and you can't fail.

CHAPTER FIVE

EFFECTIVE COMMUNICATION

When you are selling to a customer, it is very important to make a good impression very quickly. If you don't, you could lose the sale without ever knowing why. We've talked about attitude, professionalism, the way we look and feel when speaking with clients—but what about the things we *say*? What we don't realize as salespeople is that the way we speak can also become a deterrent to our careers. But there is, of course, an upside to this, because we can also use words to captivate our audience and lure them in for a quick close. A few years ago, before I wrote this book, I started looking into, quite

> It is very important to make a good impression very quickly.

frankly, ways of making my life easier. I was looking for things I could do that would help me close more deals and sell more units to my existing clients, as opposed to having to go out and prospect and cultivate more customers. While on this journey for knowledge, I came across something called *neuro-linguistic programming*.

I have learned by exploring effective communication techniques through neuro-linguistic programming, building rapport, meta programs, the use of wonder words, and the absence of toxic words. I have discovered effective methods to increase positive results.

> Effective communication is key to understanding your audience; a valuable way to understand your customer.

Effective communication is key to understanding your audience; a valuable way to understand your customer can be achieved through neuro-linguistic programming. You may have heard of NLP and considered it a recent trend, but it is not a new phenomenon; it was developed in the 1970s by John Grinder and Richard Bandler at University of California, Santa Cruz. It started originally as a study into how excellent psychotherapists were achieving the results they did, and it rapidly grew into a field and methodology all its own.

It was based around the skill of "modelling," used to identify the key aspects of others' behaviours and approaches that led them to be capable of outstanding results in their fields. In other words, it was created through studying the thinking and behavioural skills used by particularly effective and successful people.

Grinder and Bandler wanted to learn how successful people achieved that success. The study was designed to illustrate the practical application of how people think. NLP is a tool to get into the head of your client, and it can also be used to create permanent change in the thought process.

NLP is based around the idea that the subconscious mind is the key to success. The subconscious mind remembers everything; the subconscious mind also does not distinguish between real and imagined.

NLP focuses on the different modes of communication used by the general public. Everyone has his or her own learning style, and if you can identify how your customer learns and receives information, this will help you determine how to effectively communicate to your customer. People learn either *kinaesthetically*, *visually*, or in an *auditory* way. Knowing how to identify your customer's primary mode of communication is key to developing trust and building rapport.

There are many ways to differentiate each learning style. *Kinaesthetic* learners describe their experiences and thoughts by how they feel; for example, they would say, "When I sit by the fire, I enjoy the warmth on my hands". *Auditory* learners describe their experiences and thoughts by how they sound; for example, they would say, "When I sit by the fire, I enjoy listening to the crackle it makes". *Visual* learners describe their experiences and thoughts by how they see them, for example, "When I sit by the fire, I enjoy watching the way the flame flickers".

> Understanding and identifying your customer's learning style is crucial to helping you determine how to deliver your sales presentation.

NEURO-LINGUISTIC PROGRAMMING: WORDS

There are certain words that each learning type has a tendency to use.

Kinaesthetic	Visual	Auditory
Feel	See	Hear
Get the drift	Imagine	Ring a bell
Hang in there	Picture	Listen
Grasp	Perspective	To tell you the truth
Relax	Appear	Articulate
Stress	View	Resonate
Sense	Perceive	Loud and clear

NEURO-LINGUISTIC PROGRAMMING: PHYSICAL SIGNS

Each learning type has telling clues that will help you identify its learning style.

Kinaesthetic	Visual	Auditory
Eyes: Look down and to the right	**Eyes**: Look up and to the right or left	**Eyes**: Look level and to the right or left
Gestures: Rhythmic, often touching chest	**Gestures**: Quick and angular	**Gestures**: Rhythmic, often touching chin
Breathing: Deep and slow with pauses	**Breathing**: High, shallow, and quick	**Breathing**: Mid-chest and rhythmic
Speech: Slow	**Speech**: Fast	**Speech**: Rhythmically
Presentation: Towards (achieve, attain) or Away (avoid, relieve)	**Presentation**: Prefers pictures, movies, charts, and diagrams	**Presentation**: Prefers lists, quotes, and reading material

NEURO-LINGUISTIC PROGRAMMING: MODALITY

There are certain questions that each learning type has a tendency to ask.

Modality	Sub-Modality	Questions
Visual	Colour/ Black and White	Is it in colour?
	Brightness	Is it bright?
	Size	Is it big?
	Perspective	From what perspective do you see it?
	Shape	What shape?
	Dimensions	Is it Flat or 3D?

Modality	Sub-Modality	Questions
Auditory	Location	Where do you hear it?
	Pitch	Is it high or low pitched?
	Volume	Is it loud or quiet?
	Tempo	Is it fast or slow?
	Tonality	Is it nasal, rich sounding?
	Mono/Stereo	Do you hear it on one side or is the sound all around?

Modality	Sub-Modality	Questions
Kinaesthetic	Location	Where do you feel it?
	Intensity	How strong is the sensation?
	Movement	Is there movement or does it come in waves?
	Quality	How would you describe the sensation: hot, warm, etc?

Look for these words, physical signs, and modalities when communicating with your customer. This will help you to tailor your proposition to your customer's specific communication style. When you do this, your customer will receive the information you are providing in a clear, concise manner—because you are telling it in the same way that he or she processes information. Following these steps will ensure you higher closing ratios and sales—guaranteed.

> The ability to identify these words, physical signs, and modalities when communicating with your customer will help you to tailor your proposition to your customer's specific communication style.

HOW TO BUILD RAPPORT

When you were a kid, do you remember your mother ever turning and discouraging you from acting like all the other children, encouraging you to *be your own person*? She might have said, "If Johnny jumps off the bridge, are you going to jump off the bridge too?" Thanks for keeping me safe, Mom—however, you did nothing to help build my social skills, create a rapport with my customers, or improve my ability to network.

You have to find the links, the little things that create ties between you and the person you are selling to.

> You have to find the links ... between you and the person you are selling to.

The key to establishing rapport is an ability to help them feel that you are "on the same page" or are "in sync" with one another. The first thing to do is to become more like the other person by *matching and mirroring* the customer's behaviours—body language, voice, words, etc. Matching and mirroring is a powerful way of getting an appreciation of how the other person is seeing/experiencing the world.

Mirroring is just that—as if you were looking into a mirror. To mirror a person who has raised his right hand, you would raise your left hand (i.e., mirror image). In *matching* this same person, you would raise your right-hand (doing exactly the same as the other person).Timing can be important when matching. For example, if someone makes hand gestures while they are speaking, you would wait until it was your turn to speak before making similar (matching) hand gestures.

Mirroring and matching include gestures, words, speech (speed, tone, and rhythm), and breathing.

UNDERSTANDING META PROGRAMS

This simplest way to summarize meta programs is as language patterns.

Meta programs are filters that determine how you perceive the world around you, and they have a major influence on how you communicate with others and the behaviours you manifest. *Meta* means over, beyond, above, or on a different level, i.e., operating at an unconscious level. Meta programs are deep-rooted mental programs that automatically filter our experience and guide and direct our thought processes, resulting in significant differences in behaviour from person to person. Above all, meta programs can help us understand how people make decisions.

> Meta programs can help us understand how people make decisions.

Toward/Away

- The customer is motivated by either moving away from or towards something.

For example, if you ask your customer why she wants to lose weight or buy a new home, and she says, "I want to stop feeling so heavy" or "I want to live in a safer neighbourhood", both answers are *moving-away* meta programs.

Internal/External

- The customer is motivated by someone else's opinion, or he/she is internally driven.

For example, if you ask your customer what's been stopping her from losing weight and she says, "I don't know what my significant other would think about it."

Global (General)/Specific

- The customer is motivated to understand the general idea or learn about each detail.

For example, *global* customers don't want to waste time on the small print, while *specific* customers want to review every line in the contract.

Once/Several Times

- The customer has many things to consider and reconsider prior to reaching a solution, or the customer can come to the solution based on one consideration.

For example, when deciding whether or not to hire a consultant the *once* customer would make a decision on the spot based on a gut feeling, whereas the *several* client would need to read dozens of testimonials prior to coming to a decision.

Meta programs not only help us understand how our customers make decisions but they can assist in identifying the key terms and phrases to use when communicating. By understanding how your customer processes information and make decisions, you will be able to

> By understanding how your customer makes decisions, you will be able to tailor your sales presentation.

tailor your sales presentation accordingly. As a result your communication will be effective and poignant, therefore allowing you to lead the direction of the sale.

WONDER WORDS

People naturally seek the path of least resistance. Certain words (*wonder words*) have been proven to motivate, persuade, and influence more than others. Knowing these words and successfully applying them to your professional relationships and interactions will naturally and easily support your ideas/information with unlimited success.

Here are 15 Wonder Words:

- Easily
- Naturally
- Aware
- Experiencing
- Realize(ing)
- Unlimited
- Expanding
- Before

- After
- Because
- Now
- Abundant
- Possibility
- Create
- Visualize

TOXIC WORDS

Words define our lives, set our expectations, and create our beliefs. Words can, and often do, unconsciously sabotage our success, setting us up for failure, disappointment, or frustration.

Here are 10 Toxic Words or phrases to avoid using with your customers:

- Can't
- Try
- If
- Could Have
- But
- Might
- Would Have
- Should
- Maybe
- Someday

A helpful hint for both *toxic* and *wonder words*: Copy out these lists, keep them with you, and go over them until they are second nature and you are muttering them in your sleep between snores. Then you will know exactly which words to use and which to avoid when making each sales pitch.

> Know exactly which words to use and which to avoid when making each sales pitch.

With practice, you will find that picking out these words becomes second nature as you make your presentations. You will have become a master of effective communication.

CHAPTER SIX

PRODUCTION KNOWLEDGE

The importance of product knowledge is something I'm sure, by this point, I don't need to impress upon you—likely you have already been impressed. Assuming that I've done my job correctly, and you have, in fact, been reading, I won't go into great detail as to *why* it's important. Suffice it to say, if you're not constantly refreshing your knowledge, you're dead in the water.

Product knowledge is never static. It's a constantly evolving repertoire that you must have ready at any instant. Product knowledge is often overlooked and ignored as a formality, because nobody bothers with the "fine print" anymore. But that's perfectly fine. Never be afraid to let your competition load their bags onto buoyant iceberg shards and float away into isolated oblivion. They will be back when they can be, but their self-destruction is not your responsibility or even your business. Slip quietly away from the pack and teach yourself a trick or two—because the world of

> If you're not constantly refreshing your knowledge, you're dead in the water.

sales is like a cold Arctic wasteland, where even the air is dangerous and the caribou meat is never split equally.

Once a rep has a certain number of years under his belt, he can be seen lumbering into work with the slow, bored, plodding confidence of an old stegosaurus or some weathered alpha-male Savannah cat. This man has seen a few things; bosses, customers, and eager young pups have come and gone through the revolving door, and the only thing he knows to be constant and put faith in are sales, winning, and himself. His confidence is so bolstered by years of success and reaffirmation through achievement that he is utterly competent under any circumstances and *will prevail*, on the simple basis that he has so far. Generally, by this point in his life, he is either unanimously loved or hated by everyone he meets. His people skills are either sharpened to the degree of an atom—and he is succeeding in all the places he hoped he would when he was starting out—or so hopelessly overused and depreciated that everyone he meets thinks he's a jerk on sight. As I've said, this man can be very good company and an excellent resource, but be wary of looking to him as a model for your own habits.

> Product knowledge in sales is not a badge you attain. It's an ongoing process, and you have to work perpetually to maintain proficiency.

The point is that product knowledge in sales, especially in cars, is not a badge you attain. It's not like a promotion. It's an ongoing process, and you have to work perpetually to maintain proficiency.

It's not even really that hard. Most people shy away because they're not sure how to go about it. Most sales reps will just sort of float, because it's not hard to wait until your bosses tell you to watch a video and try to glean what you can from that. It may sound counter-intuitive, but the simple fact is that there is so much product information available in any "house of selling". The temptation to just coast on whatever you can learn by being in your work environment doubles, so very little actual research happens. Nobody knows where to start, and when that attitude becomes prevalent, the sales team as a body usually just *doesn't*.

It's irrelevant what industry you're in. Companies spend landslides of money generating product-knowledge training tools and materials for their employees, because they want to be absolutely sure you know what you're talking about. They create seminars and Internet courses, they write literature—they do everything they can to fill your head with that knowledge and create avenues for you to better yourself while grimly expecting you not to. They flood you this way because they know they have to; if there is information everywhere, you'll *have* to pick some of it up as you go, the same way that if you walk through a freshly painted business office you're bound to get a couple dashes of taupe number five on your elbow.

And there are plenty of other ways for you to catch up. There are consumer reports, advertisements, even documentaries, due to the simple fact that inquiring minds want to know. You can tap into and use as a resource most things done to educate the consumer.

With Internet access being what it is today, you're basically obliged to know about your products backwards and forwards, and anything less is inexcusable. Your managers will be just as unimpressed with you for drawing blanks on basic topics as your customers will.

> You're basically obliged to know about your products backwards and forwards, and anything less is inexcusable.

Nobody wants to buy merchandise from somebody who doesn't seem to know anything about it. Again, if the customers think you led them on or lied to them, they will feel insulted and overlooked.

While it's good to know a million and one factoids, you don't want to be a robot and spit out blurbs to your customers all day. First, you're going to bore them, and second, you're going to miss some of those opportunities for closing, price proposal, and prospective close of the sale. Product knowledge is easy, and it's not hard to fashion that into some kind of information sled to carry you through conversations with customers. I'm willing to bet that if you have excellent product knowledge you'll be able to outperform the other sales representatives, many of who might have loads more experience and salesmanship than you. As a new salesperson, it is your absolute right (and even heritage) to try to topple your predecessors.

You can build yourself an excellent foundation for promotion from within, or better prospective jobs outside of your current position, by learning everything you can about the things you sell. Nobody makes manager until they've mastered certain skill sets, and near-omniscient awareness of your field is a must. You will be infinitely more attractive in all aspects of your particular arena. I made management in my first eighteen months, and I finished out my career in car sales at that capacity. A big reason for that is the fact that people two levels higher than mine were stopping by my office regularly to make enquiries about the particulars of our products.

I like to take seminars. Personally, I believe that it is very important to constantly advance your education. There are a lot of ways to transfer knowledge that might at first seem unrelated (see Unique Markets), and you never know when you might come across a customer with similar interests. Any information you learn from a master of a trade can never hurt you, and friend, there are much worse things you can give to yourself than a broadened worldview.

Pay attention to brochures and flyers around your workplace, because the information that's geared toward the public is where most of your questions are going to come from. You should read and re-read anything published at a consumer level, because it will raise questions in your head that you're going to get asked about in a week anyway. You might as well troubleshoot that scenario before it happens and have an answer on the spot. Don't leave this to chance. Somebody smart once said that the day you think you know everything is the day you truly know nothing at all.

> You should read and re-read anything published at a consumer level.

There's always a bigger fish—that statement has complete resonance in sales. I don't care how good you think you are; there's another person out there who's better and acts in the exact same capacity as you do. That person might not even be in your district yet, but they very well could move in, at absolutely any time, and they are far too busy selling to worry about whether or not you can make rent. Don't let your guard down for so much as an instant. I never have—keeping professionalism close to my chest has carried me through some tough stretches and ensured longevity in a way that fast talking and big smiles never could. *Continue to seek out product knowledge* is the best advice I can give anybody on *any* topic in this field, and though it sounds generic, it is heart-stopping in its credibility.

> *Continue to seek out product knowledge is the best advice I can give anybody in the sales field.*

My background in sales spans my entire life. I was fortunate enough to have worked in my family's business from a young age, and that was a fiercely sales-driven enterprise. My father was always extremely successful in sales, and just watching him in action has done a lot to make me who I am. His natural talent was fluid; it was as if he were operating on a different plane than the rest of us. He was natural and smooth in the way that champion racing horses are, and to see him close a sale was like watching a fighter jet roll and chase in the air, effortless in its complexity. I've learned most of my techniques by watching him react to customers, and I thank him for everything he's taught me and done for me over the years.

But as I said, it's a new world, and I decided that God-given sales ability can only get you so far. I hit the books. I looked at what the customers wanted to learn about and fashioned myself into an expert on it, whatever "it" happened to be at any given time.

> God-given sales ability can only get you so far.

What you have to do is put on a different hat. Take off that salesperson hat and put on the consumer's hat. What are you looking for? I never looked at several different products at once, because that's an excellent way to confuse yourself and split your attention. I would focus on one vehicle a week, and in a five-day work week it's not hard to learn everything there is to know (or is worth knowing) about a car. I can say confidently that you're going to be a very proficient salesperson if you're an expert on your product.

IMPORTANT KEY WORDS:

- Feature
- Function
- Benefit

Keep these in mind. What is the feature at hand, what is its function, and why does that benefit you? There is a very easy-to-miss nuance of sales, in which the connection between these three things is made and the point driven home. To point at a button and grunt its name to indicate its existence is fine, but it's more pleasing to hear why it is there and how it helps your customer feel

> **What is the feature at hand, what is its function, and why does that benefit you?**

comfortable. Don't assume that person sitting beside you knows what's happening, because it's not his job to make the same leaps you are. It's *your* job to convince him that whatever you're facing him with is ideal and that he wants it. Rarely does a salesperson just use what is provided for him or her *within the product itself.*

When you are introduced to a new product (that is to say, told you are to sell something new), the first thing you should do is start with the most basic materials provided. I went for the brochures before I even went near the actual training videos. I used the things that were there to help the customer, because as I said, this is where they're going to look for information. Your job is to elaborate further.

I read the brochures inside and out, and if there was anything I was confused about, I'd go and ask somebody who knew—and there's always somebody. If it's not your senior management staff, it's your sales staff, your peers, the mechanics and technicians on site, etc. I spent a lot of time in the garage finding out how a four-wheel-drive system on a particular vehicle worked and the specifics inherent within that (for example, the power ratio between the wheels).

Once I was done with that, I went to the actual vehicle and played around with it. I pushed all the buttons, took it for a spin, opened the hood, the trunk, and the sunroof, checked out the block heater—all that fun stuff. I tried to match everything I'd learned about in the brochure with the applications in the physical layout.

That's when I went into the product books and online training courses the manufacturer had created. You shouldn't always expect these to be flawless and bug-free—be patient witfh new merchandise, because even though they've been launched with a marketing plan, the people who work the advertising are usually still getting on their feet by the time they really get into their campaign.

Regardless of the quality of your literature, it will contain technical detail, and you will have an astro-nomically better understanding of those mechanics if you have done your groundwork. You'll see a lot of confused faces in those first crucial weeks of presenting your new product, and that is precisely the time when you want to be proficient and provide intimate knowl-edge and wisdom about these new and confusing items.

Most organizations require that you achieve certain certification levels through testing anyway, so why not ace those in the process? It's honestly a no-brainer. In school I quickly realized that the students who did well at math weren't just unique and weird whiz kids with powers from above I couldn't understand—they just did their homework. That was the only difference. The majority of students did the absolute minimum and hoped for the best, while the minority of us went home and puzzled over the equations, really tried to get a grasp on them, and found ourselves miraculously in the top percentile.

Sometimes people will tell you they like math, but I don't believe that. I believe that people like proving their intelligence and validity as intellectuals on paper, and those adults who "like math" tend to do very well for themselves. Success in fields like these is just a by-product of the discovery that working on your trade yields excellent rewards. Once you get into habits like these you will be baffled by slackers and cruisers. It's all right there at your fingertips. All you need to do is to cultivate a framework—which I am doing for you *right now*. It is quite literally a recipe for success.

> It's all right there at your fingertips. All you need to do is to cultivate a framework.

In that same spirit, I went to any and all available seminars in my region. These are usually one-day deals, with free food provided, where you just sit and learn about your vehicle for free. They tell you how to sell it. I'm not joking. Why wouldn't you go? These are national product trainers. These people have been a part of it since well before the car's release, and those people who actually thought up the cars advised these product trainers directly.

And most times they bring competing vehicles with them.

When I worked for Chrysler, we were launching a new SUV that I was there to learn about. Not only did they have our company's model, but they had the competing Ford, Nissan, Mazda, and Chevrolet models, and we got to learn about what they had to offer. This is especially useful, because these guys are on contract—they're not fixed or entrenched within any company, they just float in between and make money off everybody (like Clint Eastwood's The Man with No Name character in *A Fistful of Dollars*). They come from an outside product-training company, one that everybody uses. They know your cars and all the others, and while they're obviously going to bias the presentation in favour of whoever happens to be paying for the venue, they can show you the pros and the cons of everything in the field. That was a great training tool. After that, all that's left is to bring that information to the customer.

> If by the time you get to this point you're not dangerously excited about selling your product, you haven't followed the steps correctly!

If by the time you get to this point you're not dangerously excited about selling your product, you haven't followed the steps correctly!

I liked to use outside sources as well, most of which wound up being a little unconventional. When a new truck came out, I'd talk to campers, people I knew who pulled trailers daily, for instance. I called taxicab companies and asked what they looked for in vehicles and why. If a taxicab company you know is about to grab a model for mass production, that's a fine little tidbit that you might want to pick up on before the deal goes through. Even knowing that company was *looking* at a model adds legitimacy to it. In addition, doing this increased my product knowledge and even the market in which I could sell.

Another handy thing I acquainted myself with was interest rates. Customers could come in and ask me, "What's the interest rate for forty-eight months?"

I'd ask, "Lease or finance?"

Even if they said "Both", I could tell them without looking through my papers. I just knew that it was 0 percent, or 2.9, or whatever, because I'd memorized it. Rates will change with time, but it's not a huge learning curve. Once you've attached a number to a car and know it for sure, then changing that number means you don't have to rebuild that mental association, if you can grasp what I mean. This is especially easy if you know the reason why that rate changed. As a professional, you can anticipate the need for ongoing training for existing products.

While we're on the topic of seminars, I should mention that I became a diligent fixture at most courses within my company—even those that had very little to do with my position. I took my sales training, but you could also find me at mechanics' or service advisors' seminars as well. Go on; they will not stop you. No manager in his right mind will ever discourage his sales representatives from branching out and bettering themselves (so long as that doesn't interrupt their regular functionality).

And now we're getting into what actually defines a product. It might not be long before you're trying to sell *yourself*.

If a customer was frustrated with her service (advisor), I could explain the process to her. That put me in a very marketable position. Even though I was just a lowly rep, I was working my way toward management. Those chasms become more like cracks when you already have the pattern and flow down pat. Do yourself a favour and lubricate those job transitions beforehand, so you're not thrown to the wolves when that day does come.

I even learned how to detail cars at night—after my shift was over I'd take a few hours and detail cars before delivery. I took training courses about how service advisors should handle complaints. I always interviewed exceptionally well, no matter what I applied for, and I've never been turned down for a job I got an interview for, simply because I had

> Product knowledge can come from anywhere.

an array of cognitive goods and they all carried well. That comes from product knowledge.

Product knowledge can come from anywhere, and it doesn't matter what your capacity is. Let's say you're in the furniture business. You'll want to know the fabric or strand count for your sofas. You'll want to learn about quality of leather, whether or not the sofa has memory foam, how many springs per square foot is on a particular mattress, whatever … It's all part of learning your product and excelling in your field.

I also learned what my finance managers were doing. I read all about warranty and rust protection and every other variance I might want to stick into the fray. That increased my aftermarket sales penetration, and I could load up my customers with accessories. Usually a rep will establish a relationship with a customer, sell them a car, and then send them away to a complete stranger for the options. It's a little jarring to be passed off like that. So I gave them ideas of what they might want to look for, and they were going into the finance meetings with a clear list of what they wanted to talk about. The finance mangers were impressed that *I talked to my customers,* because I could educate them in a very short period of time. Everyone loves having their work done for them, and the more at ease the customer feels, the better for the company.

> The more at ease the customer feels, the better for the company.

I have already mentioned that because of my hard-earned array of product knowledge and experience in the universe of sales, I locked myself into a management position relatively quickly. The owners and management team were aware that I knew what I was talking about, so when I came gliding in for that interview, it was really a no-brainer. It is true in almost every arena of real work and progress that you will never be promoted to a new job until you've already been doing it for about six months. There's never a need to worry about promotion when the person above you is barely doing anything—as a direct result of your skill and utter competence—and the Finance Manager position was no exception. Once you've reached that rung, everything changes, and it is always an excellent ride, even if you're just doing it for your resume. There is an endless supply of mysteries for any group of sales representatives as to what goes on above their heads. You have only to read on, dear friend, and I will pull back the curtains and show you the puppeteers and what their jobs mean for yours.

Shall we?

CHAPTER SEVEN

MANAGING YOUR TEAM

THE PHILOSOPHY OF MANAGEMENT

Look at that: "Management"—right there in big, bold letters, suspended in nothing and representing everything. It's a word that still holds grim consequence and limitless potential in my mind, even to this day, and in this chapter I will prepare you for that leap and provide perfectly coherent and reasonable strategies for dealing with your elevated position. In turn, you will give me your utmost respect (I'm sure), and we'll both come out of it as better people. So why don't I fire some upbeat wisdom at your feet, and I suppose we'll just see if you dance.

Advice on this topic is everywhere, and most of it is inaccurate—this is due to the elusive nature of management and the precise responsibilities involved. Be very careful … There's never a dull moment in the manager's climate, at least not for thinkers, and you wouldn't want to get swept away by words that don't mean anything in a book full of nonsense from a know-nothing fool. Be very careful, at all times, even with me!

I'm not like the rest of them—more like you, really, and that makes me a very dangerous person for everyone involved. I've been where you are and where you intend to be, and as somebody standing on the other side, I can assure you that everything can be all right if you allow it to be.

On any day, at any given time, the workplace can easily degenerate into a complete, hectic war zone with no clear answers and dilemma on all fronts. Managers are leaders, and when every wall has crumbled and the fires are spreading, you, as manager, are the one that everybody will look to and demand answers from. Your job is to house those answers at all times and provide immediate solutions to any problem with a cunning mix of preplanning and innovation (that is impossible to describe or outline), at a moment's notice. This mix, though shady, is absolutely essential to anyone looking to strive in the aforementioned climate. All it takes is one terrible instant for calamity to ensue, and then you're in for a ride Please understand that your employees' problems are yours as well, and if you don't think you can bear that heavy burden, then I absolutely urge you to give serious thought as to how high you want to go.

> **Please understand that your employees' problems are your problems.**

Do you think you can get by?

Do you think you can *manage?*

Wait, hold on … Let's not be rash, here. Why not take a step back and compose ourselves? There are enough terrible things in the atmosphere today to worry over. A book about sales is not one of them, and neither is a promotion (which might have occurred to you, if you've been reading carefully).

Your team must have utmost confidence in you as a leader and a problem solver. This comes easily if you've spent years maturing in your company. It is not hard for the savage masses to put their faith in a person who has accumulated a trophy rack full of awards and acknowledgements. Longstanding commitment to the team and company is always a powerful currency, because people trust that. But in today's market, if you want a promotion, the odds are strong that you'll have to go outside your company to get it.

Enter *the problems*.

There is, for some reason, a very pervasive myth that management is glamorous and wonderful. Lore trickles down through the ladder rungs, and entry-level workers whisper to one another in the night about salary components, improved hours, and job stability. Generally speaking, this myth is erroneous. There is a lot of unseen toil and after-hours work that goes in, with very little tangible reward resulting. If you were to look, you might find your managers coming in on Sundays to get paperwork

> There is, for some reason, a very pervasive myth that management is glamorous and wonderful.

caught up. I know I did. Chief among my managing woes were gruelling and onerous forecast meetings. As a matter of fact, the top 5 (or even 10) percent of your sales staff will actually make more than the managers will. The potential to make more money is often overshadowed with disgusting hassle from those lower down the ladder than you and loads of paperwork nobody seems to actually need or even want.

If your team isn't performing, or your numbers aren't where they should be, the owners will overturn your rock immediately and interrogate you. That's on *you*, friend, and if you don't have answers, then you'd better have *something*, because there is nothing more dangerous in the world than a cash-mad pack of slavering senior staff members drooling down your back and gnashing their jaws in your ear about revenue and reputation and responsibility and unemployment. Those can be very trying times, and there is no way to prepare for it other than to be the best at what you do.

You can expect to be accused regularly of causing irreparable damage to the very foundation your dealership *rests upon*, because transitions are usually awkward and executive command rarely equates to humanity (with regards to your bosses). This is unanimously true throughout the professional world at large, although in many cases I have been lucky with administration.

Take Genghis Khan for example. Genghis Khan was an excellent manager. Anyone who tells you anything different is either stupid or lazy. A brutal savage with no morals he was, indeed, but he conquered and united a realm and ended war on all sides of it. He was carried home in his casket by a parade of loyal soldiers who cut down every person they met along the way for the sole purpose of ensuring his burial place was kept secret. He is revered in Mongolia (still!) as nearly a god, and although he was a horrible baron, he exemplifies what you would hope to see in any supervisor. His subordinates respected him, he had near omniscient clarity of vision, and he was an excellent organizer.

In any case, when you are a manager, you will never get the appreciation you richly deserve, and nobody will ever pat you on the shoulder and tell you that you're handling the stress well. The only people who will understand your suffering are other managers, and they are too busy to care whether you like it or not. Your co-workers will morph into errant children who need behaviour correction, and your workload will double along with your strain.

> Being part of the management team enforces charac- ter and promotes leadership.

But take heart. I know it all sounds brutally crushing, but there isn't any reason to think it won't be beneficial. It teaches you about life and reality in all the ways that are important to everything you'd like to be. It enforces character and promotes leadership. It refines your rough edges as an individual and can really encourage you to realize the fundamental realities of life—that you can't accomplish anything without effort and that life is never easy for cowards and snakes.

The ultimate truth is that there are people who will tackle a challenge immediately because it exists as a problem, and there are those who will shirk responsibility and slip through their careers wondering why opportunity always seems to pass them by. I would rather be consistently busy and a little frustrated than spend every day of my professional life proving to myself that I am not a top-level worker and I am incapable of stepping up to the plate when the opportunity to do so arises. If opportunity does arise, do not cheat yourself out of this experience. You will always regret shrinking away from that ominous responsibility—like a skulking sea parasite that chooses to leech off the fat of larger and more powerful beasts rather than swim through the ocean depths on its own. That is a dark and frightening concept, but so is anything new and worth doing on its own merit. You can ask Carsten Niebuhr about that.

> If opportunity does arise, do not cheat yourself out of this experience. If you do, you will always regret it.

Niebuhr was a German traveler, explorer, and surveyor. He worked as a peasant farmer in his early years and later in life learned surveying. In 1760, he was invited to join a scientific expedition in Egypt. He achieved fame as the only survivor of the Danish expedition to the Middle East and India. His fame is deserved not just for survival, however, but due to the excellence of his observations, which resulted in maps that were used for more than a hundred years. He also copied inscriptions of cuneiform script that proved of great assistance to Georg Friedrich Grotefend and others in their work in deciphering ancient texts from the Persian Empire. Neibuhr's explorations of what were, at the time, distant and difficult places for Europeans to travel laid the foundation for numerous later scholars to visit and uncover the secrets of past civilizations, bringing all humankind into a closer relationship as one human family.

ESSENTIAL TRAITS OF A MANAGER

Motivation needs to be one of your main concerns as a manager. If your team is not motivated, then you are all destined to jog warily into the fog and then taper off into hard decisions about your careers and responsibilities as salesmen. Every experiment needs a control, and if your arrival in that position is the only added ingredient between the passing of good times and the coming of bad, administration will be quick to decide precisely which variable in the equation needs dropping. If you are not putting up the right numbers, they are likely to shake things up and get rid of you.

> Motivation needs to be one of your main concerns as a manager.

I had access to the budget and its continual reforming at my dealership, and with a little clever planning and total clearance from the brass, I allocated a certain amount of money toward the sales reps—and a game or two we cooked up to get the juices flowing. We would usually have one contest per quarter (four per year), and it was to celebrate a particular rep for achieving over and above sales targets. Some of the contests were team oriented.

We came up with a reward system based on points, and those points didn't just come from actual vehicle sales. People are going to strive for that no matter what, and early in the developmental process it became clear that there should be more emphasis put on the details, because that's what the company liked to see.

Reps made one point for selling the actual car, but they made two for leasing. It was three points for selling a warranty, two more for rust protection, and so on. The reps had to contribute more than simple selling. For them, the real sale became just a prerequisite for the other products, and that is precisely the sort of attitude you want to be promoting. All their main revenue had been coming from the cars, you see, so they had paid less attention to the extras. That means those extras are where a manager's focus should be, because without immediate and important gratification for the rep, these things could be easily overlooked. Seven points per deal sets a rep apart, even in that sort of contention and rivalry. A player who sells ten cars and has ten points will not be held in the same regard as somebody who sells five cars and might have twenty-five points.

> Aim to create both total competition and camaraderie between your employees.

We divided the sales floor in half and let them go at each other like wildcats. One year the opposing teams were the Flying Tigers and Top Guns. Everybody not selling as a part of the competition was a member of the flight crew. There was utter aviation obsession between the teams, with die-cast model airplanes on desks, team captains, nicknames—the whole nine yards. It was all anybody talked about. The idea was to get them so wrapped up in the spirit of things that they forgot they were at work and turned into raucous schoolchildren. It was total competition and camaraderie. There is absolutely no escaping the contagiousness of a fever borne of true fun, not when everybody's included, and that's the way it should be.

Point-based competition generates revenue and puts people on their A game. It lets you know who is doing what correctly and encourages the team as a whole to file their skills to a wicked stiletto point. Your staff will feel extremely self-confident, and you will look like a winner and a genius. Group effort to reach targets is far more effective, especially when the prize is a very expensive dinner at an extremely exclusive restaurant with the owner present. We went to Toronto, all expenses paid, with high-class surroundings and a dining experience that was a once-in-a-lifetime event. That isn't just a prize, that's a gift of experience and a story to tell. Salespeople crave those things, along with bragging rights and a feeling of accomplishment.

> Point-based competition generates revenue and puts people on their "A" game.

A large part of management is advertising, and you should always utilize the basics (newspaper, radio, posters, etc). But while keeping the standards in mind, be creative! You must always be aware that the Men Upstairs are keen to the point of fanaticism that you stay within the margins of what was set out before you, and at the same time, they long silently and desperately to see you think outside the box and create real and unique solutions. You should also be negotiating with advertising executives for things like expensive hockey tickets and air miles, and whatever other valuable bonuses you could think of that people will love but would not usually pursue on their own. That is the universal key to gift giving, and it absolutely applies to company and customer rewards.

> Create valuable bonuses that people will love but would not usually pursue on their own.

With a little haggling, the dealership and I solidified a spot on the back of the *Sun* beside the Sunshine Girl. It cost a lot, but everybody and his mother opens that newspaper directly to that picture. They use it as a measuring post for whether or not that particular issue is worth a purchase—most women do it, too. We got spots beside the stock area and weather sections. On top of that, when the local television news came on, it was brought to you (with care and support) by our dealership.

I've run a few companies, and one such organization was called Corporate Concepts and Consulting. As a national product trainer, I had to do a lot of pondering to work out what makes people buy and how to attract attention. "We think outside of the box to keep you ahead of the curve" was our slogan.

Your company's name is so important, because it's what people take away as your representation at a mere glance. You need some kind of edge. You need bright colours—red or yellow are attractive to the eye. You need "Sizzling hot sales events", "Hot deals, cool wheels"— whatever it takes. When you advertise different vehicles, don't be afraid of the lime greens, the oranges, even pinks. You're not going to sell a lot of those, but it catches people's eye and brings them in the door. That's all they *have* to do.

> A big part of cars is that they're cool, and they can be made cooler.

We always used to do up a truck with flame effects, window tinting—really go to town on it. We just did whatever looked right, and people would stop in the street to appreciate whichever vehicle we had done up to the nines. I used to butt heads a lot with the owner of that particular dealership. He said that nobody would want to buy it with "all that stuff on it", and I agreed it was unlikely, but the cue he missed is that it would really draw customers in. A big part of cars is that they're cool, and they can be made cooler. Few average customers will want a big jacked truck with flames rippling down the sides of it, but everybody wants to see it, and nobody will hold a nice paint job against you.

Sure enough, before long we started selling crazy vehicles. Never *once* did we sell one with flames (which was more than a little funny), but those trucks I mentioned would only sit for a week, tops—maybe just a couple of days—before somebody would buy them.

We made huge back-end profits on these vehicles, because they had step bars and dual exhaust and tonneau covers and whatever else. The only thing the customers didn't want was the stickers. It costs $100 to $150 to letter them up, and that's not much investment to move a car. Anyone in the car business knows you want to move a car in thirty days, but sometimes cars will sit in the lot for two or three months, even a year or more, so why not just take a chance? Put vinyl on it! You're not changing the actual vehicle, and that stuff peels right off. This is your job, comrade, and if you're not willing to move and shake, then I'm really not sure what to tell you.

Focus on third-party selling. Give your sales rep one hour, and when he comes in and wants a price proposal, your two-minute drill is to ask the sales rep as many qualifying questions as you can. This way, you can see if the guy did his job and what the customer's buying mind is. If buying and trade are his main focus, then you can structure your deal for that. Do some role-playing with your employee. Role-playing is very important, because this is where you set out and critique what your rep is going to say to the customers.

> Role-playing is very important, because this is where you set out and critique what your rep is going to say to the customers.

Part of your job as a sales manager is to help your representatives mould a reality around the customers. You can create an alternate universe where everything is convenient for the sale and the representative is in cahoots with the customer. The salesperson can disappear into his manager's office and return with good or bad news, depending on what will make him or her the most money. These situations are exceptionally malleable.

The sales rep can go to the customer and say, "Sorry, my manager is a little tied up right now with a customer, but if I could get X amount of dollars for your car, do we have a deal?" Then your rep knows what she is closing to, and that is drastically useful information. Then she can bring that information back to you and let you structure the deal accordingly. If the customer is only shopping, you'll give him the lowest price on his new vehicle, and the highest price for his trade. Have your seller say to the customer: "*If I could do this*, do we have a deal?" If he says no, she says, "Thank you very much for your time, and I'm sorry we couldn't

> A sales rep should never make promises; by doing so you only box yourself into a corner.

find more common ground—but please, try to get this deal anywhere else. If you can't get this deal, come back and see me, and I will do what I can to make this happen for you."

A sales rep should never say "I can do it" and should never make promises. *Never* box yourself into a corner. We do not make guarantees for the same reason that triage nurses didn't in times of war—because there is a very fine line between a promise and a lie, and they can quickly become the same thing if your buyer returns and angrily demands to know why he can't get his best dollar for a car you lied to him about during your last proposal.

It is very controversial to centre out your top performer, and many people will tell you not to. It is always up to you as a manager to make the big decisions, and using that formula and creative licence, I *will* absolutely point that salesperson out at a meeting. I want everybody to know who is at the top of the chain on that given week, month, or whatever, and for good reason. You can expect a pack mentality in your reps, the same way you can in Scandinavian gray wolves. As a form of government for that pack, you have the authority to decree who is in the front—and this is a vital position for humans to be in, for whatever reason.

> Dale Earnhardt was never happy with just finishing the race, and your reps won't be either—if you do enough positive reinforcement.

It appeals to our primal side, the one that is jealous and angry at anyone who manages to pass us in line. We are all driven to get somewhere, but for most of us that somewhere is vague and blurry. For that reason alone, any time we see somebody else getting somewhere we could have gotten to first, it raises contempt and competitive frustration in the hearts of the rest of us. You would hope for humanity's sake that a successful businessman's peers would applaud him wholeheartedly for his achievement, and you will find that most people will congratulate this person, but if you watch their eyes closely you will see pride burning in the *vitreous humour,* just past the pupil and barely before their festering arrogance.

Pride is a deadly sin, just like any other, and that makes it just as useful for both you and for your salespeople. If Johnny sold eighteen cars last month, then slam that down on the boardroom table and let them deal with it. Nobody gets into car sales and has any sort of continuance by deciding at the start of the month that they want to be ranked as "pretty good". Dale Earnhardt was never happy with just finishing the race, and your reps won't be either—if you do enough positive reinforcement for these people who are generating serious money for you. Nobody who's made any sort of dent in anything aimed for the middle. If you're just barely paying your bills in a sales-oriented workplace, then you likely won't manage to keep that job—those are not the people I'm talking about. I'm talking about the movers and shakers that actually comprise the team. They will want that top spot. They will also want the bonus five-hundred-dollar individual-standout-performance award you may or may not drop in the lap of any seller who found a big enough foothold to shove himself ahead of the pack (if temporarily). And that's leaving out completely the entitlement side of it.

> Don't be afraid to centre out a member of your sales team who has done outstanding work.

So don't be afraid to centre out a member of your sales team who has done outstanding work. Put that person in front of the rest of them and discuss the high points he or she has been hitting, and then have an open forum about how those skills apply to everyone and how easy it can be to win and succeed if you follow the format and make the customer happy.

> It's important to never be negative to your sales team. Always be positive.

At least twice a year you should have a meeting where the owners or the general managers aren't present. Tell your staff that you like to make sure that they are happy with the way things are, and you want to take their feedback to the owners. "Just tell me all your complaints. It's in confidence. I won't finger anybody. I'm going to raise general concerns." It lets them know you're concerned about their well-being, and it gives them more trust in you, because they feel you're going to take their opinions to on high and have them dealt with. Beloved leaders never snub their people, and it's important to never be negative to your sales team. Always be positive. If you get flak from your boss, it is a huge tenet of leadership not to bring that to your employees. If they have questions about product knowledge, address them right away! Make resources available for them. Let them know you're on their team. It is impossible to make everybody happy, but if you try, you really can get most of them.

This brings me to the hiring process. You're going to have to hire and fire, and that is an eventuality that will catch up with you sooner than later. A great manager has instincts about people, as does any salesperson, and you must trust that above any resume or portfolio. Personally, I have absolutely no respect for resumes.

You cannot sum up a person on a page of paper, and you must never forget that a person's past accomplishments can only count for so much. Draw your foundation of opinion from your *personal experience with that person*. Anybody can do well in school and get cushy jobs if he has the capacity to do put his head down and memorize whatever is necessary, and he knows some of the right people.

See people for what they could be. See them for what you think they might be and for what they aspire to be. Having said that, never hire somebody who is bad *now* but could be good *later*. People will disappoint you in that way, and it is not your job to raise pups. It is your job to maintain a strong staff of good sellers, and while you're better off holding out hope for success and personal achievement, bad news comes from expecting people to change. If somebody's a bad apple who won't respond to you, just get rid of him, because he will poison your environment and cause you stress later. If he's not interested in making you happy and following direction, he's not interested in being there, and you simply don't have time to take passive orders from new people like this.

When I got my first job as a salesman, I was living in a car. I was at a crossroads in my life, and everything around me had fallen to pieces. I felt like I was

> We truly only ever have what we create for ourselves.

at the end of the line. The roads I had been counting on had seemed to end all at once, without warning. The world can be a very unforgiving place, and I learned then that we truly only ever have what we create for ourselves. I had maxed out all my credit cards from living in hotel rooms, and I was forced to keep my clothing in the back seat of my car and everything else I had in my trunk. This was a very nice car, mind you, and it was designed for optimal seating comfort— however, it failed me in recreating the experience of a house with plumbing and heat and enough space to move my legs or lift my arms above my head. I was too proud to turn to my family for money and too stupid to ask for help, so I did what most people like me would do in a situation like that: I suffered.

I didn't last very long in that situation.

I spent my last night of that drudgery in a lot beside a park. I rose with the sun and went outside to stretch my legs. It was the middle of November, as I recall, and while I was scraping the frost off my windshield, I noticed a section of newspaper blowing by. Open to anything at this point, I picked it up and looked over the classifieds. There was a help wanted ad for a car dealership. There wasn't much left to lose; I needed money badly, and I'd known a few people that made handsome living in car sales. So I made the call.

> Sometimes enthusiasm is all you need.

I got myself an interview for a few hours from then, so I drove to a nearby McDonald's (I'm not joking) and changed into my only suit behind a stall door. I shaved in the sink there, touched up my appearance, and went off to my interview. I had no background, no resume, and no references—an utter void where all the commonplace standbys should have been. I shook my interviewer's hand, sat down across from him, and said, "I will be your next Wayne Gretzky of car sales, if you give me a chance."

I talked my way through the interview, and he passed me on to the used car sales management. He told me he liked my approach. He didn't know I was sleeping in my car at that point, and neither did anybody else until years later. All he knew was what I showed him, and what I showed him was complete enthusiasm about having that job and a willingness to bend over backwards to get it.

Ultimately they gave me an aptitude/self management skills test, and they faxed it off for me. Three hours later they called me back in. Then they told me what the compensation plan was, what the hours would be like, what would be expected of me, etc. The sales manager turned to me and said, "Your aptitude test came back. It said you could walk across water and not get wet. When can you start?" That's a direct quote, and I can still hear him saying those words to me and answering every question I'd been asking myself for weeks.

> All he knew was what I showed him, and what I showed him was complete enthusiasm about having that job and a willingness to bend over backwards to get it.

I started right away. I didn't have a choice but to succeed. I showed up early every morning and stayed there until night. My managers literally had to tell me to go home. The other sales staff were complaining about me being there so much. I ate, slept, and breathed my job. It wasn't long before I got my licence, and in my first week I sold a car. My second week, I sold another one. Learning as I went, with absolutely no room for error, I was the top salesperson at that dealership, with a grand total of eighteen cars that first month. Again— no resume, no formal sales training other than my background helping out in the family business, and nothing but personality and sheer willingness to contribute on my side.

> Find somebody who wants and needs to succeed. That's always your best bet.

So throw that resume in the garbage. It's a great reference point for contact information—what area someone lives in and their name—but attach no validity to that paper as it equates to any person's true capability and spunk. Any arrogant rube that thinks he can skate through an interview based on his past achievement is going to have to move a little father on down the line to find a job. That person hasn't done anything for you *yet*, and if he acts like he has, pitch him. Find somebody who wants and needs to succeed. That's always your best bet. Use your instincts, and you'll get top guns across the board.

People will have their own critique of your managing style, and they will also talk about you when you're not around. These people may be your friends, but they are also your employees, and you should understand that venting is part of the working progress. Don't let anything anybody says deter you from the goals you've set for yourself and your team. If you allow them to change your style, they will try to change it in a way that is beneficial to them—not to you. Keep your game face on, stay professional, and don't ever let your personal life and feelings get in the way of managing your team. If you can keep that in mind, you'll do well no matter what, and everything will start to come together for you.

> Stay professional, and don't ever let your personal life and feelings get in the way of managing your team.

CHAPTER EIGHT

CHARM

I have spent an exorbitant amount of time reassuring you that charm is not a crutch and will not get you by. I stand by that theory, and I have never been willing to contradict myself in any circumstance. I still contend that the best/only way to ensure success is to produce results unflinchingly at every turn. However, it is important that you realize the gravity of charm and all it has to offer.

Charm can build a person up. A charming person can make another's day better and create a fond memory (if one is lucky). At its essence, charm is about making people feel better, because happy people are easier to deal with. You could imagine it as a sort of defence mecha-nism, I suppose. It can be a way of anaesthetizing people into a state of calmness and joviality. Essentially what we are doing is learning how to sell cars—but we

> At its essence, charm is about making people feel better, because happy people are easier to deal with.

must always remember there is a line between charm and manipulation.

The difference between bettering yourself as a salesman and trying to force action from other people is a big one, if thinly divided. If your goal is to manipulate, then your charm will never blossom the way it could, and people will be able to taste that in your speech and action. Charming salespeople mean well and progress through obstacles the best way they can. Manipulative people back customers into corners and cut their throats when all other avenues are exhausted. This type of behaviour is identified quickly, and if the obvious moral dilemma isn't clear to you, then you should at least remember that it will absolutely obliterate your referral rating.

Charm is a disastrously mislabelled beast. Nobody knows how to explain charm, but everybody knows what it looks like, and in the interest of getting a grasp on the concept, you might start with that. It is an ethereal spectre that defies natural law and the mechanics of perception. Charm is something that very nearly escapes title, the sort of enigmatic sensation we see as a natural talent that one might have from birth, as though a gift from God that is intrinsic to that person. Some people just have it, in the same way that some kids are just better at reading than others, or the way chess champions are never friends with professional soccer players because they weren't ever meant to be. Be it genetics or otherwise,

> We must always remember there is a line between charm and manipulation.

we are positive that this is granted rather than attained, and that not only have most people missed the party, the collective *you* have somehow been selected for eternal awkwardness and will always be mocked at parties for lack of social skill.

And there you have the heart of the problem: people who are "not charming" continue to be that way partially because they don't think they can do otherwise. Most people are very nervous about the way they come off, because the world is not kind to losers, and nobody wants to be that person who is unanimously disliked and completely unaware of it.

> People who are "not charming" continue to be that way partially because they don't think they can do otherwise.

Most of us will attain charm through bold and funny conversation, for just an instant, then shrink back into ourselves and watch how the people around us are reacting. It is in this action that we lose it, and in this moment we are, again, "not charming". The reason for this should be obvious if you've taken the time to observe the steps carefully.

Confidence is the key: freedom from inhibition—or, more accurately, freedom from self-imposed social restraint. Charming people are not worried about how they come off, while at the same time they hit each and every polite and fun social cue correctly. They do this because it is who they are. It appears as if politeness and correctitude are coded into these people's very genetic makeup; they have a somehow preternatural sense of what is and is not pleasing behaviour. They do not shake hands firmly and laugh at jokes and maintain eye contact because they are worried about you not liking them or because they have been taught that is how you make friends. They do it because it just makes sense; it's instinctive. That is why we are usually so wary of charming people. They just don't seem real enough.

I suppose I should say that when they make an attempt, it reflects these ideas, but usually charming people are not fully aware of themselves or even what they're trying to accomplish in their disingenuous way. Nobody is completely smooth and confident, or at the very least they shouldn't be, and with that basic primal knowledge stemming right from the dawn of evolution, we take a step back and investigate. Of course, that's only when it's being done wrong.

When it's done right, words like *art* and *beauty* leap to mind, as opposed to *attempt* and *failure,* and *sleaze.* When a person has managed to analyze the world around them well enough to mirror back all the positives and very few of the negatives—really and truly incorporate that into their personality—it is a wonder to behold, and I'd recommend it to anybody. We must keep in mind here that we are not talking about changing who you are. We are talking about the way that you present yourself and the effect you have on the people around you. We're talking about business and everyday social interaction. We're

> Take a look at the way that you present yourself and the effect you have on the people around you.

talking about people wanting to be around you for your personality, and taking interest in the things you are interested in. We're talking about life and emotion and patterns of behaviour that are or are not conducive to your personal achievement and work-related success. You, the person inside, never change— we wouldn't want that.

> You will find your behaviour start to shift, as will the behaviour of the people around you.

But if you pay attention and take time to ponder these ideas, you will find your behaviour start to shift, as will the behaviour of the people around you. You might find more people seeking you out for conversation, and invitations to dinner will start to arise more than they did before. You can *make* yourself "charming", whatever it means.

I have seen a genius sale or two in my time, and I have had the joy of meeting a great many slick people, but in the interest of applicability, I'm going to assume that everyone reading this book does not have my background. So, with the spirit of fresh perspective and communicable tactic behind me, let me spin you a gripping tale of real-life *charm* in action:

THE CASE OF THE HOT ACES

I once witnessed a convenience store clerk being charmed out of a pack of cigarettes by a homely street person in a brown coat. It happened one gloomy afternoon on the wrong side of Peterborough. Ashkata was the clerk's name, and while I never caught the moniker of her smiling would-be suitor, it never mattered and nobody questioned him. He was slick and charming and beautiful in all the right ways, even though you'd never look twice at him if he weren't speaking and most of us in the store that day were originally repelled by his unkempt appearance.

"Say, darlin'... What kind of smokes you got over there?" he asked, having swaggered calmly and smoothly up to the counter, his interest wholly on the stock and not at all on the attractive late-teen East Indian cashier. "Got any Hot Aces?"

She furrowed her brow in consternation. He had her now, and it was inevitable. I just wanted to buy a can of diet Pepsi and a pack of gum, but I could see before she could that this might take a little longer than your usual transaction. So I faded into the background and pretended to peruse a magazine, listening intently all the while.

"Hot Aces? No, I'm sorry, sir; I don't believe so." She shook her head cautiously.

"No, eh? Well, that's a shame. Hot Aces are my favourite brand, ever since I was a kid. My grandpa used to smoke 'em. Taught me a lot, that guy." Ashkata knew she should be ending the conversation, but she wasn't sure why or how—and if those two foundational elements are missing, then what's a girl to do? Something intuitive nagged at her insides—she'd seen the same look on countless customers—but she was interested and didn't really have much else to do.

"Taught me this trick," he added, resting an elbow on the counter. He lifted a pack of cards from his coat pocket and fanned them out in front of her. "If you don't got any Hot Aces, well then, I suppose those'll have to do." He nodded toward a pack somewhere in the middle of the wall behind her while he shuffled, just a glance and a tip of the hat, busy with other things and wholly uninterested. "Them red ones right there— that's just the one I meant. Thank you … Ash-kat-ah? Is that how it's pronounced?"

She smiled and shrugged. "Most people don't get it right."

He grinned at her. "I suppose that doesn't surprise me." A moment passed between them while he held her gaze. Just a brief second, utterly meaningless should it be seen on camera or from a distance—but it was there, and like all important moments, it seemed to stretch on and wrap itself around everybody involved. He spoke first, still holding the cards. I noted that the cigarettes had made their way to the counter. "Now, if you wouldn't mind, lovely, why don't you point to one of these here cards."

She nodded and complied, leaning forward a bit, her eyes gleaming and interested, unable to keep from smiling. "That one," she indicated clearly, and she drew that card at our mystery man's urging.

Holding that card toward her, not looking at the face of it, he went on. "Now, look what it says. See it?" She nodded, and I wish I'd been paying less attention to her expression and more to what happened next. She placed the card back in the deck, he shuffled, and then he pocketed the cards. Ashkata was a little bewildered, but he just grinned.

"This your card, sweetie?" he asked, lifting the cigarette pack and revealing her card underneath it. She squealed with glee and excitement, clapping her hands, asking how he had done it. "Couldn't tell ya if I tried. It's magic." He wiggled his fingers in the air and bobbed his eyebrows, and she giggled again. "Hot Aces are a little cheaper than these … I don't know if I got enough. You wouldn't mind helping me out, would you, Ash-kat-ah?"

She glanced around and paused, chewing her lower lip. Eyes wide and mind racing, she made sure the other patrons hadn't caught the exchange and that I was totally engrossed in my magazine. Then Ashkata nodded her head and pushed the pack toward him. "Go ahead," she grinned.

"Well, that's awful generous of you. I'll make sure to come back and see you." He nodded his thanks and swiftly pocketed his spoils. "Have a nice day … and stay out of the cold."

And then he was gone, evaporated, like a modern-day phantom materializing and dematerializing whenever he deigned to converse with mortals. His escape was swift and silent, not too hasty and gleeful, but not slow and celebratory either. He flashed a genuine smile to the girl at the register, and the bell above his head heralded our last glimpse of a rare beast. Something special. Something altogether foreign, and both she and I somehow felt a species branch away from him. It was one of the few times I've ever felt that I was in the presence of genuine charm.

Looking back, now, I like to think that if he and I had spoken, I could have bested him and managed to come out of the exchange on top. But when I think of the look on her face, combined with what I remember feeling bubbling up inside myself *standing adjacent* to the actual conversation, I am not positive of anything.

WHAT HAVE WE LEARNED?

In the case of the Hot Aces, we are taught some very important lessons very quickly—beyond those about general conduct in society and why it's important to set goals and progress beyond the point of conning teenaged store clerks for cigarettes.

The thing I recognized as a tactic almost immediately was his initial disinterest in her. This is important, because it plays off the insecurity most people secretly harbour, as I stated early on in this chapter. People are skittish creatures and generally dispassionate about social interaction with strangers, because they are used to not getting approval from outside sources. Rarely are people told in their day-to-day lives that they are doing a good job or told in an inoffensive manner that they are attractive. Mostly compliments are cons, set strategically in place to do precisely what the man in the brown coat did to

> Rarely are people told in their day-to-day lives that they are doing a good job.

Ashkata. We are used to feeble attempts from people we don't like to get things out of us, women especially, and as a whole we tend to be very wary. In order to get something out of somebody, you must first assure them that you *don't* want anything from them, that you are all right on your own, and their assistance would be appreciated but is not required.

You will also note that the cigarettes were in transit almost from the moment he walked in the door and started plying his social wares. He maintained his adversary's attention and kept his goals under his hat while Ashkata played into his waiting hands. Not only did she allow him to have the thing he wanted, she *gave* it to him, because she liked him that much. What makes charm so important is that if you do it right, people will be proactive in producing the things you want without even being asked.

> What makes charm so important is that if you do it right, people will be proactive in producing the things you want, without even being asked.

Note that the man in the brown coat was friendly, and he warmed to Ashkata immediately. Charming people like you right away. They want to be your friend. They will try to win your affection out of genuine interest, and when they look at you they see a person with a brain and a soul and a beating heart rather than an obstacle or a representation of what you have to *give*. Some people, however, will not be able to recognize this display of social competency, because they lack that

126

capacity in themselves, and it is essential to remain confident whether or not you can walk through a room and be unanimously liked. It won't necessarily depend on whether you're hitting your cues right.

I saw an interview with the cast of Monty Python once. They talked about a live performance that they were sure would lay waste to the crowd. Opening night, the people roared, and the comedy troupe beamed with pride. Fuelled with all the confidence of a successful career and the growing feeling of a true hit on their hands, they stormed on stage the next night and ran through the same routine.

> Charm is subjective; as hard as you try, you can never really *force* anybody to feel it.

It flopped.

They were utterly baffled. There was no evidence of differentia between the two showings and no lighting or sound calamities to speak of. Absolutely beside themselves with self-doubt and looming dread, they were desperate to understand. After seriously pondering and weighing probabilities, as a group they came to a decision:

The first night, it was "funny". On the second night, however, it was "not funny". This is true of any ambiguous feeling generated from another's action, because *charming* and *funny* are very much alike in more than one way.

You can be charming at one party and not charming at another, and you'll have to take that in stride and ignore it as a sign of anything. It does not mean that you are losing your edge, and it does not even reflect badly on you as a social person. Charming and funny are subjective things, and as hard as you try, you can never really *force* anybody to feel either. It is true what they say: you can't make anyone do anything, and in brief instances this will ring true. If people are, for whatever reason, uninterested in seeing what most other people tend to, then they will invariably overlook it. You will find that, because of our society's foundational beliefs, many tactics will work well with a wide variety of people, and this is due in part to the shrinking of the world via television and the media. North Americans have a tentative unspoken, shared understanding of what works and what doesn't, and the majority of us (having seen that label) will ascribe to it wholeheartedly. The same way that one celebrity will be fashionable one month and inexplicably undesirable the next, we accept what we are told, because it is easy and we believe there are people better positioned to make those judgment calls than we are.

Charm is mythical, but only in the sense that it is actually a myth. There is only that activity which works out well, and that which doesn't—and if you seek to control that outcome, you will fail eventually. You must realize in attempting charm that it is something that you suggest to the world, and people will take

> You must be willing to realize that every person and situation is unique. So, then, is charm.

what they want from it. And that is why charm is not one sure-fire equation of action that you can simply have down pat in your head and coast on perpetually. You must be willing to realize that every person and situation is unique. So then is charm.

Take your cues from your customers, because they are the people you're trying to appease. If they are loud and boisterous, match that, or at least turn up the volume on that section of your personality. You are reaffirming that their behaviour is acceptable, and what's more than that, you are accepting it. Those are two leverage tools you should always have at hand; you should never leave home without them. People who laugh loudly and speak grandly do so because they feel the need to, because it is their adaptation strategy for the world around them. The same way that the Canadian lynx's coat grows dense and pales in winter (*The Encyclopedia of Animals: A Complete Visual Guide*, Cooke, Dingle, Hutchinson, McKay, Schodde, Tait, Vogt), you should morph and contort to accent features for better adaptation in your surroundings. The person you're dealing with will change your atmosphere just as well as any weather or physical building (or at least they should, if you're trying to be charming).

Take your cues from your customers, because they are the people you're trying to appease.

Having said all that, you should try to accomplish the standbys. Eye contact is key, and that information is well documented. Nobody will take you seriously if you refuse to maintain eye contact and cannot withstand the visual scrutiny of monstrously intimidating people without flinching. Never allow yourself to shrink under intimidation, because intimidation is very much akin to those ethereal emotions we were talking about.

Nobody can make you feel intimidated, any more than you can make them like you—and while that sounds discouraging, it really isn't at all. There is no feeling or sense that hangs in the air around you or them. There is only what you generate for yourself, and nobody can impose on your mental state. Knowing this gives you power, and people who have confidence in their power will not *have* that power over you. Otherwise they wouldn't depend on their daunting presentation to carry them through every situation. Remember how that's wrong? In case you haven't been reading carefully, this sort of presentation and attempted intimidation is another kind of charm. It is not useful to you in any way, but knowing how to combat it is never a detriment.

Charm is not a gift from Shiva, and it is not just an overall smoothness. It is *adaptability*. It is the ability to blend in appropriately with whomever, and a big part of that is picking your crowd and gearing yourself toward that mould. The man in the brown coat didn't walk into an Ikea store and try to scam a couch out of somebody; he went to a dishevelled convenience store on a bad street and fleeced some poor kid out of a pack of smokes she probably wound up paying for.

Charm is adaptability!

You need to be genuine! A big part of being charming is doing extra things to be nice. Take extra time and be positive; if somebody needs you to slow down or go over something again, assure them that you're not worried about it. Tell them you don't get to leave until after five o'clock anyway, so an extra fifteen minutes working out the details isn't going to bother you. Take the time to assess peoples' needs and wants and wishes, because charming people are interested in others, and they want to know what makes the world move.

Charming people are smart, and a great way to look smart is to be well rehearsed in your product knowledge. There is a chapter on this particular point, so I will leave it there, but I *will* mention that a surplus of information never hurts in the ongoing battle to achieve legitimacy. *Illegitimacy*, of course, would be detrimental, because not knowing or being able to find product information can disrupt your would-be groove. Try to spend twenty minutes a day (less time than you likely spend socializing) rereading brochures and testing yourself on motor specs. Your smile and desk will look a lot more convincing.

> Take the time to assess peoples' needs and wants and wishes, because charming people are interested in others.

Look people in the eye, but don't stare. Shake hands, but don't grab them. When somebody is talking, let them talk, and take the time to commit what they're saying to memory. Make their wants and needs important to you. Pay attention. Talk to them about their personal lives, and get a better idea of where they're coming from. Laugh at their jokes, give honest compliments, and don't complain to them about your problems. Face them fully when you're speaking, ask questions, and make a joke when the opportunity arises—not before. Be friendly. Be polite. Be the person that everyone wants to talk to but nobody can find. Suggest to them with your mannerisms and tone that you are a good person at your core and that you are generally satisfied with your life. As I said, every situation will vary, and depending on the encounter, you may or may not win them, but if you build off this foundation, you'll never have far to go. Just be natural and stop over-thinking. Know that you as a person are valid, and everything else will just flow naturally. You might also find yourself smiling more.

> Know that you, as a person, are valid, and everything else will just flow naturally.

CHAPTER NINE

TELEPHONE TECHNIQUES

If I didn't make it clear in Unique Markets, you can't rely on door traffic—not if you want a steady flow of business and a successful record. It's amazing how much dealing salespeople do over the phone—or at least they should—because lunch breaks and trips home during kids' soccer practice are prime times to try getting hold of someone and "get this thing in the bag", as a friend of mine used to say.

You should always be professional over the phone, because the fact that people are not there in your office doesn't make them any less real as customers and potential money. What I meant by that (of course) was a potential sale, with mutual benefits on all sides of the fence. These people are *people*, my friend, and they will expect the same person on the phone that they saw/will see in your office. It was always astounding to me when a rep would pause from our conversation to quickly brush off customers over the phone and hastily wrestle

> Always be professional over the phone.

appointments out of them. When customers call, not only is it like they're walking in the door, but they're walking in the door *to see you specifically*. This brings us back to professionalism and treating customers correctly. They are your number-one priority, and whatever it takes to establish that is a bargain at twice the price.

If you're doing a good job of generating interest in yourself through the public eye, you will be getting phone calls from people you don't know. Until they've seen you face to face, they have no idea what you're like. Many people will try to make the customer commit quickly to a personal meeting so that they can woo said customer in person. This is a very backwards way of thinking. You can understand it—the same way that you could understand why my friend Dan's daughter jammed a peanut butter sandwich into his VCR to "see what it looked like inside"—but anybody who knows better has only to shake his or her head and chuckle. You are not mysteriously "off the clock" when you are called, and everything we've discussed in terms of interpersonal behaviour and professionalism still applies.

> If you're doing a good job of generating interest in yourself through the public eye, you will be getting phone calls from people you don't know.

"Hello Mr./Ms. Customer, thank you for calling ABC motors! My name is Gordon O'Neill. How may I help you?"

You'll find that working the phones will be a good way to generate customers when the dealership is slow and door traffic isn't what it used to be (not that it ever is). Get on the phone; call people you've had before. Maybe there are people in that Rolodex who have lease maturities coming up, and they'll need to re-sign, or lease a different car, or *buy* one—whatever the case may be. Maybe they've had service inquiries. Some return customers might need repairs done in the shop. You can call and follow up with them, see how their service went, if they have any questions, etc. If they haven't made your repairs, maybe it's time to turn in the vehicle or flesh out some exciting options for them.

You'll want to be checking for sales leads. People will be calling the dealership because of all that fancy ad work we've talked about. Check with your receptionist, and stay on top of it. If you're the first to get the call, that's an easy prospect. Oftentimes in sales, you'll feel like some sort of back-alley detective, chasing down tips and following trails. People will make you chase them—expect it. But don't try bullying them into commitment, and never attempt excessive calling and e-mailing. Your job is not to make them commit—your job is to make them *want* to commit, and if you allow them to lock you into

> **Your job is not to make them commit—your job is to make them *want* to commit.**

the position of hounding, sleazy car salesman, then it's over, because they can easily justify brushing you off once you've made that transformation. The same way that most people will hang up or yell at telemarketers, if they feel you are transgressing upon their personal live, a boundary will have been crossed, and you will be more assailant than actual help. Selling will be very difficult to do under these circumstances, and there will be very little wiggle room.

Telephone work is delicate, because that person on the other end has no idea who you are or what you look like. He will read into your words tenfold what he normally would, and that includes inflection, tone, vocabulary, and so on. He's trying to feel you out from the word go, but that is fine, because you are a seasoned professional with a knack for counter-intelligence. You need to know that if this person hangs up the phone and feels anger or offense, you've blown it, and that's one less customer. You want to get him into the office, because an angry customer can be passed off to management or even another salesperson. There is still money to be made as long as he is physically present.

> Keep in mind that this is a gift. You didn't have to fight the floor to get this person; he called looking to talk to somebody. He found you.

Keep in mind that this is a gift. You didn't have to fight the floor to get this person; he called looking to talk to somebody. He found you, and you are now his only contact at that dealership. Why would he call anyone else? Remain confident, and don't fumble the ball. Titanic amounts of money are spent yearly generating and updating scripts geared toward telephone conversation. These scripts are in place to help you deal with customers at a distance, and if you're not willing to use those assets, then I would never want to be in a life raft or a foxhole with you. Most salespeople will shy away from scripts, because they feel silly and wonky trying to accomplish proficiency with them. When you've got a piece of paper with predetermined lines written on it, and a living, breathing, unpredictable person on the phone, you will inevitably try to match what exists on the page with what is transpiring in your ear.

This is wrong for obvious reasons, and I somehow feel that we've already discussed them very recently, if not a single sentence ago. They are *scripts* only in name, and you should memorize key lines and greetings rather than upgrade those words into crutches. They are for *reference only.* They are not gospel, and they are not trying to be. If, after honest effort, you find they hinder more than help, then congratulations! You are an extremely proficient talker, and your flavour of personality is bewitching, though I am sad to report that you likely don't respond well to multiple types of stimuli at one time.

> They are *scripts* only in name, you should memorize key lines and greetings, they are for *reference only.*

A motto I have always found extremely reliable is this:

Don't lie to bring them in, but don't tell the truth to keep them away.

I am completely unashamed to tell you that is the art of selling. You are creating what the Canadian legal system refers to as an "invitation to treat", and there is a difference between covering up facts and not mentioning them until later. When you have those people in your office, *then* reveal the things they might not like, in the dealership, where things can actually happen. Your likelihood of saving a sale goes up dramatically once everyone involved enters your office.

> Take your time on the phone, and gather up whatever information you can. Ask when you could sit them down in the dealership. Always close to an appointment.

Take your time on the phone, and gather up whatever information you can. First, get the person's name. If they ask specific questions about the vehicle that you are unwilling to answer, tell them that you're not positive about the specifics. Ask for a number you can call right back in a couple of minutes. Now that you have their phone number, have your information ready and double-checked for when you call them back. Mention everything positive you know about the vehicle. Don't lie to bring them in, because they'll just find out later, and nobody needs that sort of business. Just quickly and casually tell them everything you know to be good about it, and then mention that you don't have it all in front of you. Ask when you could sit them down in the dealership. Always close to an appointment.

Don't talk payments over the phone. Tell people that in order to give the best deal, you'll need a day or so to get hold of your manager and work something out. Ask, "When can I book an appointment for you to come in and see me? I'll have the numbers ready for you, and I can give you a price proposal."

Never talk trade information over the phone, either. Everybody who comes to your door has an absolute gem of a car—be prepared—and they will expect top dollar for their flawless diamond in the rough. They will want you to commit over the phone, and you won't want to. Tell them you need to check with your used-car manager, and you'd love to know when they could come in. Again, you're closing to an appointment. You can't do what you want over the phone, and you want to be in control.

I like to change my voicemail greeting every day, if only because it makes me look punctual. Try to sound bubbly and professional on your answering machine, and don't let it vary too much. The funny/cute answering machine message doesn't work in the business world.

"Thank you for calling ABC Motors. You've reached the voicemail of Gord O'Neill on Tuesday March the thirteenth. I'm sorry I can't take your call

> Be polite, pleasant, and positive.

right now, but if you leave your name, number, and a brief message, I will try to return it in the next few business hours. If you need assistance immediately, please dial zero, and you will reach my assistant, so-and-so."

Be polite, pleasant, and positive. Let yourself redo the message if you mess up partway through, and speak clearly. I would never insult your intelligence by suggesting you stay away from ums and ahs, because clearly, if you've made it to the end of this book, you are a competent person (and probably, by now, already a selling master).

Be advised that your phone-ups are tracked and logged by management. Supervising the group is absolutely a responsibility of The Men Upstairs, and they will know when you improve. That will mean even more leads, with likely more success and money attached.

Should you follow the steps outlined in this chapter and all the rest, you just might accrue a reputation for effective salesmanship, along with all the worldly possessions you can wrap your arms around. Likely, you'll enjoy a lengthy reign at the top of your class and be showered with respect and accomplishment and currency. They might even call you "The Professional Salesperson". And when you've accomplished all you set out to and you've seen every mile marker, well ... I suppose there won't be much left to do but write a book about sales.

> If you've made it to the end of this book, you are a competent person (and probably, by now, already a selling master).

"A winner is someone who recognizes his God-given talents, works his tail off to develop them into skills, and uses these skills to accomplish his goals."

-Larry Bird

Services Available
SELL MORE NOW!

Gordon says: I am available for speaking engagements, workshops, coaching, and private auto sales events. Hire me!

Speaking

Gordon's speaking presentations have captivated thousands of sales professionals in the financial services, insurance, and commissioned-sales businesses during the past 14 years.

Gordon's engaging presentations are a must for all sales professionals. Because of his extensive background in sales, Gordon knows the top three priorities of anyone working in the sales field:

- How to increase sales
- How to attract new customers in a cost-effective manner
- How to promote customer retention

He effectively provides practical, proven strategies on meeting these major concerns. His speaking style is uniquely informative, yet captivating, and he always leaves his audiences wanting more.

Specializing in keynote topics such as sales techniques, sales career advancement, effective communication, customer retention, and marketing strategies, he brings useful, motivational, and thought provoking presentations to his audiences.

Through his business successes, he draws lessons from fascinating real-world examples, educating and supporting decision makers towards success. Having certification as a life coach and expert in Neuro-Linguistic Programming, as well as Six Sigma (Black Belt), and Lean Management, Gordon designs his captivating presentations to teach his audiences to utilize proven strategies and make the best business decisions.

Gordon's background and career achievements have shaped him into the sales expert that he is today, and he has helped reinvent the careers of many successful salespeople.

Listed below are several topics and workshops that could help make your event an enormous success.

Keynote Topics and Workshops

We have numerous speaking topics and workshops below to pick from to help make your event an enormous success. However, we also know that every event, conference, convention, team-building application, and/or sales rally is unique and different. Therefore, we will custom build a presentation designed specifically to meet your needs—created for you, your audience, and your overall desired message.

Any of these keynote topics can be set up in either a presentation or workshop style.

Effective Communication. The art of conversation using neuro-linguistic programming

Explore effective communication through neuro-linguistic programming (NLP): building rapport, meta programs, wonder words, and toxic words, too. NLP is an effective methodology to successfully deliver your message.

We give you the skills to consciously deliver positive messages to your customers while helping you to be cognizant of "toxic words" that will ruin your sales proposals.

Whether you are trying to make your sales team communicate more effectively or make certain that they are successfully relating to your customers, this seminar is right for your team.

Takeaway: You will leave this workshop feeling connected to your customers, and will be able to use the techniques learned in your everyday business life.

You will learn the skills to build relationships with anyone you come in contact with, which will allow you to increase your market share, close more deals and, therefore, boost your sales numbers.

Sales Survival. Your complete guide to a career in sales

You will gain a vast knowledge of everything that relates to selling.

Whether you're in auto sales, real estate, insurance, financial services, or commissioned sales, this is a must-see presentation.

Gordon delivers this program in a unique and thought-provoking style, engaging the whole audience with extensive hands-on training.

Together, you will work on developing and implementing new strategies that will make your sales soar through the roof and will generate a positive client base.

For this program, Gordon will work directly with your company's management team prior to meeting with the sales force.

He will then build a dynamic presentation and/or workshop that is focused on your business's challenge and current market state.

Takeaway: You will learn how to close every sale, exhibit professionalism, find unique markets, retain customers, acquire new clients, and create a value-added sales force—rather than just being a product seller.

Recession Proofing

It's the topic in the forefront of everyone's minds—how to stay afloat, and even thrive, in difficult times.

In this seminar, you will learn the necessary tools to succeed in any market and any economy. Learn the tools to build long-lasting relationships that will generate sales, guaranteed. You will also learn the art of marketing your brand, or your personal services, in a cost-effective manner.

Takeaway: Learn how to work less and sell more, even when times are tough—for everyone else.

Automotive Sales 101

We teach this program in two parts.

The first stage of the program is dedicated to the sales force.

They will learn how to: do a proper "walk-around presentation," overcome objections, show professionalism, and close every deal.

The second part of the program focuses on the business office, where our tried-and-true methods will increase: insurance sales, aftermarket products, cash conversions, and extended warranties.

Takeaway: Regardless of whether your office is the showroom or it has a door and a nameplate, if you work in a car dealership, we will show you how to attract customers, retain customers, generate sales, and close deals.

Coaching

The terms Executive Coaching, Life Coaching, Career Coaching, and Personal Coaching all refer to a process of helping anyone to achieve his or her full potential. Coaching may be applied to work-related or personal goals, and it may be used with an individual or with a group of people working as a team.

Life coaching is an effective way to enhance your personal and professional level of performance and to realize the best version of who you are. Whether you are an executive, a sales professional, or a worker in an entry-level position, we can help.

From time to time, you reach pivotal moments that help define your career and your life as a whole.

These moments will make or break your future, and they are vital to your existence.

Sales Survival is your solution.

Gordon is a certified life coach and has the years of experience and necessary skills to help.

Together, you will work directly with Gordon and his team of certified life coaches to realize your full potential and live your best life.

Coaching is a highly successful method that can help you realize your goals and aspirations for both your business and your personal life.

Ask yourself these questions below and if you answer "Yes" to any one of them, then coaching is right for you.

1. Are you feeling boxed in, frustrated, bored, or even complacent? Do you have the desire to take your business or career to the next level?

2. Has your income stopped growing? Are you having difficulty achieving the next income bracket?

3. Do you feel that you deserve more in life than what you currently have?

4. Do you feel that your career has hit a major roadblock and that you have the skills to achieve more but are missing that key ingredient for success?

5. Have you outgrown your current position but don't know what the next step is?

6. Have you lost the passion and enthusiasm you once had for business? Do you want to find a way to really love what you do?

7. Does your current career or business put a strain on your personal life?

Private Auto Sales Events

Want to boost sales at your car dealership? Want a sales plan that closes more deals than you can count? Want a winning marketing strategy that will build customer relationships and promote customer retention?

HOST A PRIVATE AUTO SALES EVENT!

What is an auto sales event, you ask? An auto sales event is a private sale that offers a chance to boost your sales volume considerably. This type of private sale creates a huge impact, often generating the equivalent of a week's worth of sales in one single day. The private sales event gives you an opportunity to sell while you present a limited, intimate, and exclusive event for your most loyal customers, as well as those customers you may not have seen in awhile.

Many car dealerships spend tens of thousands of dollars every month in an attempt to attract new customers into their showroom. They spend money hand over fist on advertising and marketing, while completely missing a hidden sales strategy.

It's easy: target your existing customer base as an ongoing source of repeat business. Why do so many car dealerships miss out on this seemingly obvious sales concept? Most dealerships do not have a sales system in place that measures the effectiveness of their advertising. Put simply, they are unable to effectively track the Return On Investment (ROI) for their marketing dollars...

WE HAVE THE SOLUTION FOR YOU! Host your own private auto sale.

Our events can be described as:

- EXCLUSIVE: Your existing customer base is targeted for a one-day private sale.

- PROVEN: This sale is designed to welcome a car dealership's bread and butter, its sales and service customers.

- TARGETED: It is marketed effectively by using high-impact direct-mail invitations. Exclusive invitations are personalized, by using the customer's name and a new vehicle image based on their current vehicle.

- EFFICIENT: It is an effective way to advertise your newest products, by showcasing your latest launches on the invitation.

- TWICE AS EFFECTIVE: In addition to the invitations, personal *live* phone calls are made by our call centre to all invited customers, inviting them to book appointments. We provide scripts, training, and encouragement to your sales staff to call all their recent buyers.

- INTERACTIVE: Customers can RSVP on their own, through the web or by phone.

- LUCRATIVE: Be ready to sell your weekly sales volume or more in just one day!

- HIGH ENERGY: Events are fun filled. Your return on investment is typically much higher than with traditional advertising (newspaper, radio, mass mail).

So, get ready to attract proven customers into your dealership, using marketing strategies and sales techniques, and take the opportunity to close more deals than you can count.

For more information on any of these services, please visit:

www.sales-survival.com

NOW AVAILABLE

The Sales App

Your complete guide to a career in sales, including payment calculator, sales tips and closing strategies.

Available for download at the Apple App Store & Google Android Market

ABOUT THE AUTHOR

Gordon O'Neill is one of Canada's leading sales and marketing experts in the financial services, insurance, and commissioned sales fields.

Through speaking engagements, Gordon has captivated thousands of sales professionals in these fields.

Audiences find Gordon to be motivating, inspirational, and thought provoking. By drawing lessons from fascinating real-world examples, he educates and empowers decision makers. As a certified life coach and expert in neuro-linguistics programming, Gordon easily provides the necessary knowledge to make the best business decisions, utilizing his proven sales strategies.

Gordon was born into business and started his sales career at a very young age. When he was only 18, he started a career in automotive sales at a large Chrysler dealership in Toronto, where he joined a team of more than 20 salespeople and quickly went from young upstart to top salesperson after just one month. Gordon maintained top status until moving into management.

Gordon's unique career achievements include automotive sales and leasing, business management, financial services, insurance, tool and die making, construction, wholesale manufacturing, retail, and landscaping. His background has provided him with the rare opportunity to relate to many different business fields.

Gordon also holds certifications in Project Management, Lean Management, and Six Sigma (Black Belt).

As a manager, he was rated in the top one percent of all business managers in Canada.

Gordon is married to the love of his life, Shannon, and resides just north of Toronto in the heart of cottage country. He is active in his community as a volunteer firefighter and is involved with a specialized search-and-rescue unit. He has a passion for living life to the fullest, and for anything with an engine.

Gordon's background and career experiences have moulded him into the sales expert that he is today, and he has helped transform the careers of many very successful salespeople.

For more information about Gordon O'Neill, go to:

www.sales-survival.com

INDEX

A

B

C

D

E

managing your team 113
matching and mirroring 69
meta programs 62, 69, 70, 146
mindset 53
mirroring 69
modalities 68
modality 66, 67
modelling 62
motivation 99

N

national product trainers 85
natural market 43
negotiating 102
neuro-linguistic programming 61, 62, 146
new job 89
new product 82, 84
niche markets 38
NLP *See neuro-linguistic programming,*

O

objections 25, 26
open-ended question 48

P

people skills 76
phone-ups 142
positive thinking 53
potential clients 48
product information 77, 131
product knowledge 4, 11, 51, 75, 76, 78, 80, 86, 88, 89, 108, 131
Product knowledge 75, 78, 88
professional salesperson 7, 143
professionalism 47, 49, 61, 80, 136, 148
Professionalism 38, 47, 147
promoted 89
promotion 39, 76, 79, 89, 95

Q

R

S

T

U

V

W

Y